PRAISE FOR *FROM SHOR*

C000182438

"This is a volume of truly beautiful poet
internationally orientated, personally pα
spiritually life-giving."

JAMES HAIRE AC MA PHD DD DLITT DUNIV
Emeritus Professor of Theology, Charles Sturt University, Canberra, and Former
President of the National Council of Churches in Australia

"In reading the beautifully crafted and emotionally honest poems and prose of
From Shore to Shore, Pamela Ferguson reminded me why I love the quiet,
pristine beaches of Ireland and Indonesia.

They entice us to slow down, to amble in the calming beauty of nature, to
linger over horizons that stimulate our curiosity, and to plunge into the freshness
of the ocean.

Some, I know, prefer to jet-ski over the surface, but this book is an invita-
tion to explore the depths beneath the waves and the emotional depths within
ourselves, the shimmering colours as well as the darkness.

The range of themes addressed is expansive: nature's eloquence, God's still
small voice, the silence that envelops visitors to Auschwitz; the gift of children
and the legacy of grandparents; the confusion and enrichment of living in
different cultures; the joy of belonging and the pain of separation; peacemaking
in a divided community and protecting the planet; the wisdom-quotations from
Vincent van Gogh and the life-revealing art of Rembrandt.

The Christian spirituality pervading *Shore to Shore* resonates with the
rich classical Celtic tradition of 'the land of saints and scholars'. Today it is
experiencing a global renaissance because it offers a way of encountering God
which re-energizes the human spirit through the gift of Jesus Christ.

I'm not in the habit of reading a book twice, but for this compelling volume
I will definitely be making an exception."

VERY REV DR KEN NEWELL OBE DD
Minister Emeritus of Fitzroy Presbyterian Church, Belfast
Recipient of the Pax Christi International Peace Prize (1999)
Former Moderator of the Presbyterian Church in Ireland
Author of *Captured by a Vision*

"Against a background of rich and diverse experiences from different cultures that have enriched her life, Pamela Ferguson has produced this sensitive and faith filled collection of poems and reflections. It makes inspired reading. I recommend it to all who have a pilgrim soul."

REV DR RUTH PATTERSON OBE
Author & Director of Restoration Ministries, Northern Ireland

"I have long appreciated Pamela Ferguson's creative abilities, both visual and verbal. Nevertheless, reading her book has been a revelation of hidden depths both in the art of storytelling and in poetic expression. Her skill in blending these together, each complementing the other, has produced a finely-balanced text that makes for easy and enjoyable reading.

Each chapter begins with a cluster of poems around a single theme, inspired by an encounter or observation or significant life event. Each is carefully crafted and is wide-ranging in its use of poetic forms and language. This provides us with a window into her world and allows us to share her sense of beauty or wonder or pathos or joy which, for her, are clearly not mutually exclusive.

The second half of each chapter tells her story in prose form, or provides a meditation from Scripture on the themes addressed in the poems. The unifying theme that emerges is the providential care of the loving Father who is also the Creator of all things. Pamela's poetry has evoked the dazzling wonder and beauty of creation; now we see the same God caring for his broken creatures and intervening with perfect timing to bring about his purposes.

This brief appreciation can only give you a tiny glimpse of the treasures that you will find in *From Shore to Shore*. You will experience delight at the lightness of touch in Pamela's use of language, be inspired by the tales of tragedy and triumph, strengthened by her experience of the faithfulness of God, and nourished in your innermost being by the confirmation that the words of Scripture are true and also relevant to our daily lives. Read, enjoy and be blessed."

DR ROY MILLAR FRCS
Bible teacher and author of *Come and See: An Invitation to Journey with Jesus and his Beloved Disciple John*

"I wholeheartedly endorse this outstanding book of poetry and reflection. I loved and savored every word. Several of the themes moved me very deeply and I know many will find encouragement and emotional-mental strengthening and healing by reading them. Our model of the 'purpose driven church' complements the wonderful global view that the writing so beautifully communicates. The words reflect a life lived in a spiritual awareness of what Eugene Peterson calls 'a long obedience in the same direction.'"

JANICE FLINN
Ministry Team, Saddleback Church, California and
Former Assistant Executive Director, Foundation For His Ministry

"This is a feast of a book! The author has drawn on the experiences of a lifetime, lived on three continents and in many nations. The joys and sorrows of family life in these settings, with cross-cultural adopted children, illness, bereavement and elderly relatives are all recorded in evocative poems, followed in each section by further reflections in prose. The amount of content this provides could serve as a twelve-week study and reflection on issues of life, nature, family and society. But the more poetic reader will concentrate on the poems, dipping in to savour the word-pictures and reflections expressed so beautifully by the author.

So whether as a poet or a pastor, there is so much to glean from this book. Read, savour and enjoy, and give thanks to the One who transforms earthly lives into vessels of glory and grace, as they are offered to Him."

FAITH FORSTER
Poet and Pastor and Co-founder of Ichthus Christian Fellowship,
London and Overseas

From Shore to Shore

From Shore to Shore

Life in God's Global Kingdom
Reflections in Poetry and Prose

PAMELA FERGUSON

Pam
with love

RESOURCE *Publications* • Eugene, Oregon

FROM SHORE TO SHORE
Life in God's Global Kingdom: Reflections in Poetry and Prose

Resource Publications
An Imprint of Wipf and Stock Publishers
199 W. 8th Ave., Suite 3
Eugene, OR 97401

www.wipfandstock.com

PAPERBACK ISBN: 978-1-7252-5251-6
HARDCOVER ISBN: 978-1-7252-5252-3
EBOOK ISBN: 978-1-7252-5253-0

Manufactured in the U.S.A.   01/07/20

For
Suzanne, Jay, Rhys and Ruby
Paul and Corah
and
Jim
all a part of life's poetry and drama

Contents

Acknowledgements

Thank you to all who have found their way into these poems as people who have inspired me and helped to extend and shape my view of life, by their faith, insights and compassion. All have shared different stages of life's voyage with me. Some have been there from the very beginning; some have already gone ahead and reached another shore.

A few people are identified in my reflections, but many others, unnamed, have been an important part of the events I've touched on, both near to home or in distant countries. I appreciate deeply those who have given generous words of encouragement at moments when they've been most needed. All of you have enriched my life and made poetry possible.

I want to thank especially Ros Critchlow, Rosemary Millar, Eileen McClenaghan and Rosey Bell, whose friendships stretch over many decades. Thank you for reading imperfect early drafts of poems, being so positive, and believing my work should be published. Also, thank you to our sisters, Eileen, Rosie, Janet and Ann for their comments on the final draft. Over the years, the faith and love of all these strong women have encouraged me beyond words.

Nor can I forget my earliest friend Ian Mitchell, a third culture kid like myself, born just a few days before me in the mission hospital in Nigeria where his father worked as a doctor. With his wife Pamela and my husband Jim, we have exchanged ideas and experiences over a multitude of coffee cups.

And how can I begin to express my thankfulness for Jim, who has partnered me in all the challenges and joys revealed in these pages? He has been my sounding board for every poem, from the earliest drafts to the final crafting. All along he has believed in me and spurred me on. We have been a team in all our tasks, relating to our family and those whom God has led us to in many places. It was Jim who suggested I add a reflection to each chapter of poetry and his input in contributing ideas and in formatting the document has been invaluable. He has worked meticulously with me on the project of this book, which for us is another voyage of faith, an opportunity to share something of our lives and our thinking with the wide family that stretches from shore to shore.

A Chapter Guide

From Shore to Shore is a book of poetry written over many years, arising out of personal experience of events, places and encounters. The poems are arranged in twelve chapters, each an individual short collection with a prose reflection added that links the poems to personal narrative, biblical meditations, and observations on life events.

My overarching theme is that God is present and invites us to join with him in his work on the earth today. He communicates with us in all of our life experiences, those we enjoy and those in which we are severely tested. The book celebrates in poetry and prose how, as Isaac Watts wrote in his famous hymn, "Jesus shall reign" and "his kingdom stretch from shore to shore."

Much of my poetry is a response to the world of nature. Chapter 1 begins with poems written on various coasts, mainly in Ireland, followed by a reflection on my childhood experience of a sea voyage and adjusting to life in a new place. I was born and spent my childhood in Nigeria where my parents worked with what is now called Mission Africa, and this awakened my curiosity about the world.

Living and working in various countries has provided the stimulus for much of my writing, and there is a special focus on this in chapters 2–5. Eleven years in mission in Asia enabled me to witness something of the growth of a strong, independent church in Indonesia, and also how Christian communities in Indonesia and

Japan express their faith in a way that respects and reflects the local culture. I also experienced living through the troubles and the attempts to bring peace and integrate a divided society in Northern Ireland. Coming to Ireland from Nigeria as a third culture kid gave me a lifelong empathy with the stranger or newcomer in social groups or in society. Today we have the opportunity to welcome and befriend those who have arrived as refugees and newcomers from many countries.

Some of the poems and reflections in chapters 2 and 3 arise from events that I can only attribute to a remarkable outworking of circumstances pointing to God's involvement in our daily lives. The story unfolds of how we came to adopt our daughter, and then our son, in two different countries. Chapter 5 links past and present across five generations and three continents, and reflects on how Jesus introduces a radical new meaning to the concept of family.

Confronting challenges of life and death is explored, particularly in chapters 3 and 7. Issues of family coping with autism, teenage crises, illness, dementia, separation and early death are just a few of the struggles that many have to endure; hugely demanding but also times when we have been most acutely aware of the presence of the God of compassion in the midst of life's disappointments, suffering and grief.

The poems in chapter 6 are meditative responses to some Bible passages and themes that have been a great source of strength and encouragement to me. I discuss creative ways of communicating biblical stories and truths from my experience of living and working in different overseas contexts.

In chapter 8, I focus on two of the paintings of biblical scenes by the master artist Rembrandt van Rijn and speculate on how his choice of subject might have been influenced by specific events in his family life at that time. Visiting some places in Israel linked with biblical events prompted the poems in chapter 10.

The poem in chapter 9 was written after a visit to the Auschwitz-Birkenau Memorial and Museum. I reflect on the genocide of the Jewish people in the holocaust and how God's mission involves speaking out against injustice and working for peace. I pay tribute to the remarkable contribution of the writer and Nobel Peace Prize winner, Elie Wiesel.

Chapter 11 returns to the theme of the natural world, and our responsibility to care for the earth and protect it from exploitation. I consider how Jesus connects images from nature in his teaching about overcoming fear and anxiety.

Chapter 12 is an extended poetic reflection on the experience of Jesus during his temptations in the wilderness. It was written during the six weeks of Lent, and includes some suggestions on how it might be used as a resource in the context of prayer and worship or group Bible study. It helps us enter imaginatively into the natural environment of the wilderness and the Jewish Old Testament roots of this time of preparation for Jesus, leading to his ministry proclaiming the new kingdom of God in word and in deed, culminating in his death and resurrection.

My hope is that the poetry and reflections that have grown out of all kinds of challenges and blessings will help to show that the person God made each of us to be, living in the strength of God's Spirit, contributes in a small but unique way to the fruitfulness and growth of God's Kingdom.

The prophet Zechariah speaks of the Messiah and his kingdom: *See, your king comes to you . . . He will proclaim peace to the nations. His rule will extend from sea to sea and from the River to the ends of the earth* (Zech 9:9–10).

1

Coastal Path

If one truly loves nature one finds beauty everywhere.
—Vincent Van Gogh, letter to Theo, 30 April 1874

BEACH RUNNER

Race
      wind-jostled
            on the wet shine of the shore

Leap
      with the light-and-shadow
            from the cloud-spin

Splash in the spray
      of the sun-jeweled rain
            in the rush of light
                  chased by the wind

COASTAL PATH

Scattered on the sky this evening
the wildflower colors of banks and hedgerows—
sea pink, violet, glint of fuchsia, rose—
strands I glean and fasten
in a binding of hope,

but the clouds are clay on the horizon,
a flint-grey fence,
an ashen screen closing
that will not mold to my demands
or open at my bidding.

Rain like charcoal strikes the headland,
smudges the lough as boats race to shore.
Quickening pace, rethinking the route.
Below me the cliff, a tangle of brambles,
berries in bundles, hard green knots.

One day when ripe I'll stop to pick them,
watch as black-red juices blot.
Hand in hand we've clambered over rocks
and looked as crabs come crawling out
from nooks in blue and amber pools,
clawing, spying out their prey,

but today I keep on walking;
though storm clouds follow me
I carry close to me
my gathering,
my cradling of hope.

ISLAND IMPRESSION

Sculpted on Jurassic rock
time-freeze life form
the world forgot

Etched on the arch of a hidden cave
time-locked language
earth people lost

Carved on a Celtic cross of stone
serpent-coil
at the foot of a child

Inscribed on the vellum of my heart
Word of life illuminated
treasure saved

Engraved on the hand of the Son of Man
the human name
Creator's image

Imprint of nail.

FALLS

Shafts of rain
driven by hammering wind
skim across a thin panel of sky
and swipe the roofless church
that sits astride a mossy hill of graves,
a lifespan scored on every slab,
a whole life hidden in every name:

Coughlin, O'Loughlin, Callaghan, Flynn,
Droney, Mahoney, Flanaghan, Glynn,
Cleary, O'Leary, O'Looney, O'Shea,
Heggarty, Healy, O'Dwyer, O'Dea,

echoes of names in streets below
on dripping signs on streaming walls
of huddled shops with half-shut doors,
village cleaving to a bridge
straddling the Inagh Falls

whose water
slashed by gleaming rocks
spills and whirls
like beads of jade and amber,
jasper, quartz and jet,
a votive gift, an amulet,
torrents of joy and anguish
bursting and roaring onto the surface
of the bronze and copper mirror
of the river

opening flat into the valley
where wind-bitten trees with budded branches
charting years and generations

bend and beckon to hill and walls,
to family lines in hidden rooms,
to all of life
the river that flows
and falls and leaps with grace and swirls
beyond the rain-scored stones:

Coughlin, O'Loughlin, Callaghan, Flynn,
Droney, Mahoney, Flanaghan, Glynn,
Cleary, O'Leary, O'Looney, O'Shea,
Heggarty, Healy, O'Dwyer, O'Dea.

THE LONG WINTER

On the west coast
between Kilfenora and Kinvara
with the ancient fortress of King Guaire
the bare fingers
of the crouching trees
are blue in the mist,
the wild flowers of the Burren
have not dared to raise their heads
in this late spring

and in pools of rain
on a karst meadow
at Poulnabrone
these mighty stones
have lain and borne
five thousand winters,
a portal tomb
for whom or how or why
is scarcely known.

In the glens of the north east
the stone walled farms of Dalriada
mourn their loss,
the April lambs
their skilled hands tried to save
were born and dead by evening,
slain in a harsh and bitter blow,
whole flocks entombed, a silent ruin,
in graves of drifting snow.

ATLANTIC EDGE

Into the blue dome of sky
blue as the ocean
they soar like white arrows—

gulls, fulmars ride the wind
light on ledges
high-wire act of the giant hippodrome
rock carved by sea and storm

and from their nests high
on juts and ridges
kittiwakes swoop down,
trapeze on crests of waves

and over a burst
and fling of spray
the aerial dance
of petrels

while gannets circle, spy and plunge
to seize the prize
deep, deep
below the surface of the water

as we perch on the cliff edge
strain
lean hard against the gale
to view the vertical drop
the curved expanse
its bands and layers
of sandstone, silt, shale
and fossil fauna
mapping eons before human existence

and crane
to watch the performance
matchless flamboyance
of birds.

Heights of blue
blue as the depths
mystery in air and ocean

like the word
spoken in the beginning
wind hovering
over the face of the water
the first day breaking
the world
layer on layer awaking

at the wild
wondrous cry
of the Bird.

BITS FROM A BEACH (a child's collection)

Light is the feather
heavy the stone
carefree the driftwood
wind-tossed the cone
strong is the flint tool
fragile the bone
the shine on a seashell
fragments brought home.

Days that are gathered
like bits from a beach
drift in with the tide
toss out beyond reach.
In wind and on waves
we are safe on the sands
we're strong as he holds us
kept by his hand.

AT THE FOOT OF THE MOUNTAIN

Wave on wave of turquoise silk
fold, roll and spill
in fans of scalloped lace;
the push and pull,
a polishing of pebbles,

the crunch of feet on shingle,
memories drift like shells on a skin of sand,
lip-smooth curves,
the scrape of saw-tooth edges,
the slip and shift of silk and lace.

In the crook of the harbor elbow
boats nudge and nestle
as castles crafted, journeys traced
swirl in the tide,
the prints of feet and hands.

Behind us on the mountain shoulder
a yellow shawl of gorse unravels,
scorches, blackens,
a flecked tweed of heather
flares and smolders

as snakes of smoke twist
and funnel in gaps and cracks
in gleaming granite and in the fronds
and fiddleheads of bracken
flame-tongues fume and wrestle,

flash and snap and tunnel back
between the boulders,
steadfast rock through tide and fire,

the spume and spark, salt and ash
of years our lives have spanned.

In time the mountain will renew her finery,
bloom more and more,
while the sea spreads a bridal dress
day after day
in a tryst on the newly washed strand—

my hand in yours, holding you close,
unwavering on the ageless shore.

REFLECTION

Early voyager

A long time ago, three children boarded *The Aureol*, leaving the tropical sunshine for the cold regions of the north. Only mother was there, as father still had some tasks to finish at the college where he was working at the time. The vessel was one of the last passenger mail boats that voyaged between West Africa and Liverpool. We stood on its deck and watched our metal trunks being lifted by a crane and dropped into the ship's hold with the rest of the cargo. Soon we felt the huge craft pull out on the murky green water, while the quayside and skyline of Lagos gradually receded, and I said a silent, ceremonial goodbye to Nigeria, the land of my birth and home for nine years. I sensed that those two weeks on *The Aureol*, our circle of light leading our family back to Ireland where our parents came from, marked an important passage from all that was familiar in Africa to new discoveries on another shore.

Third culture kid in new surroundings

As fair skinned children in Nigeria, two auburns and one blonde, we knew we were seen as very different to the children we lived among. I didn't realize that on arrival in Northern Ireland this feeling of strangeness wouldn't just disappear. In the streets around my grandparents' home in Belfast where we spent the first few months, I was made aware of the differences between creeds and cultures when children whispered and pointed and avoided other kids on the way to school because of different uniforms, linked with words like Catholic and Protestant. How could they be so separate, I puzzled, when to me, we were just Christians in contrast to the ju-ju charms and animal blood sacrifices that we'd seen in West African animism? Everyone else seemed confident in an environment in which I felt foreign. I didn't know then that I was experiencing what later would be well documented, the reactions of a third culture kid (two cultures coming together to make a third).

In contrast to the colorful surroundings of African markets and tropical vegetation, we had to get adjusted to the shock of dull, wet city streets, and instead of the security of home school, face the tension of stern classroom teachers and the erratic behavior of unruly pupils.

Then we moved to a rural town in South Armagh where we set up home in a rambling old manse heated by open fires. Furniture was gathered quickly from auction houses, and for a while the living room was used for table tennis until our parents could afford the carpet and complete making the curtains. Our dad, a church minister who had spent thirteen years serving in Nigeria, couldn't expect home luxuries, but I never heard him or mum complain about not having enough. What was there to complain about when we'd seen such poverty and malnutrition, queues of hungry children on our veranda each morning waiting for a glass of fortified milk, with leg ulcers to be attended to? We'd watched and helped our mother as she prepared the drinks and bandaged wounds, before starting to teach us at home. We didn't have running water or electricity at the mission house, and we had to use a pit toilet in a hut outside. What we now had was luxury.

The little three-teacher village school we attended, that seemed so remote to city people, was our new center of civilization. Kind, friendly children welcomed us, the newcomers, as rarities and curiosities, introducing us to their games, like the art of juggling two balls against a wall while chanting rhymes, or playing hopscotch on the flagstones. When our teacher asked the class to suggest a title for creative writing, I offered a storm at sea, but because we were an inland community, the idea was rejected. Not only was a sea storm considered too far from everyone's experience, but any connection with the political storm about to rage in Ulster was, at that point, far from all our thoughts.

Countryside and coast

But to me the seascape was familiar. Weeks spent on a voyage on the ocean, as we travelled to this place called home, had exposed us to enormous waves as we held on to heaving decks, exhilarated though not alarmed, for hadn't we heard stories of how St Paul had been rescued from shipwreck on his missionary journey? The Titanic account was not on our radar then, although the shock and sensation of the event were in living memory of our grandparents, as they told us some time later.

The wonder of the oceans and distant horizons had become part of my inner landscape. Life was a journey into the unknown: we could expect storms, but there was always a captain, fog horns, a tug boat and a pilot to guide us safely into ports. Childlike faith grew from seeing courage and constant gratitude, the enduring life-attitude of our parents, neither of whom was a risk taker by nature.

My father, the youngest of eight from a farming family, loved the countryside and the shores of Ireland, and one summer managed to pack all seven of us (a fourth child, a toddler then, plus granny who came to live with us after grandpa died) into our little Morris Minor. The luggage, complete with dismantled wooden baby cot, was tied to the roof rack of the car. It was a healthy lesson in learning to get along together, as well as a test of faith for 'travelling mercies', in the words of dad's frequent request in prayer. It was also our first introduction to the coastal towns and beaches of Ireland.

In my teens I loved exploring the countryside along a lane just outside our home, discovering little valleys, woodlands and winding streams. It was on this peat land, among multiple mosses and bog-cotton, that I blended nature, beauty, hope and prayer.

But there was rising political and community unrest that began to bewilder and unsettle us. Just as winter's snow came first to the hills on the border, so did the conspiracies, ambushes and distrust of neighbors. When the lane I loved to walk became an 'unapproved road' and was barricaded to prevent the traffic of weapons across the border, I sensed that the evil of armed conflict threatened to destroy Paradise Lane (known to everyone else as Bog Road). Our townland took on an increasingly ominous atmosphere, but we were able to maintain normal life at the girls' high school, despite the early start with three buses to catch in the mornings from our house to the town, then to the city and after that to the school gates.

It was at this school, now called Armagh Royal, that I met my very good friend, Rosalind. As an avid reader of the Anne books by L.M.Montgomery early in life, I'd prayed as I faced the challenge of another new school, that I'd find a friend who was a kindred spirit like Diana was to Anne of Green Gables. In Ros, I found not only a kind, adventurous school companion, but a life-time close friend whose insights, practical wisdom and sense of fun I have always enjoyed and valued. She and her husband Steve Critchlow have spent their lives in mission in God's global kingdom.

Shores in poetry

I have lived in Ireland for quite a few years now, and walks by the coast are a vital part of my existence, physical and spiritual. The poems in this chapter were written on various coasts mainly in the north, east and west of Ireland.

Island Impressions is a meditation after a visit to Iona in the Scottish Hebrides, where a Christian community is based in the medieval Abbey on the site of a monastic community founded in 563 by the Irish Saint Columba (also known as Columcille, meaning 'dove of the church'). Columba of Iona had ties with Comgall who founded a large monastery in Bangor, County Down, where I now live. Bangor monastery then became an important center of learning and Columbanus, pupil of Comgall, travelled extensively, establishing monasteries in Switzerland, France and Italy after the collapse of the Roman empire. By the time it was raided by the Vikings, Bangor monastery had spread Christian spirituality and learning all over Europe, establishing more than one hundred monastic schools in many countries.

Bangor was referred to at that time as a light to the world, and is clearly marked on the *Hereford Mappa Mundi*, the most famous medieval map of the known world. Along with Iona and Bangor-on-Dee in Wales, it was regarded as one of three leading centers of Celtic Christianity. I think of the Irish and British missionary families I grew up calling my aunts and uncles in Nigeria as standing in this long tradition. Today Bangor Worldwide Missionary

Convention provides the opportunity every year to hear from international Christian leaders.

Coastal Path was written at a time when I was waiting for medical test results. This path is part of the Bangor Christian heritage trail as it's from this coast that the monks used to set sail. I go there often and the colors and movements of sea and sky are ever-changing.

The Long Winter was penned on an April break to the Burren, a limestone area in County Clare famous for a wide variety of spring wildflowers. It was just after the severe snowfall in 2013 that devastated many farms and halted the arrival of spring.

I wrote *Falls* in the same late spring. The names, except for Cleary, are all ones I noted in the old hill-top cemetery in County Clare. I added Cleary, one of the first recorded surnames in Ireland, because it is the Irish form of my maiden name, Clarke, from my father's family in County Cavan. In this way I identify with "the river that flows" in the poem.

Bits on a Beach was put together with my grandson Rhys when he was nine, asking him to suggest words to describe the natural objects he picked up as we went along the beach.

At the Foot of the Mountain began as a walk along the shore at Newcastle beside the rugged and beautiful Mourne Mountains. This popular beach evokes memories of childhood, youthful friendships and romance. It was a hot summer's day and a gorse fire had started on the mountainside. I was aware of a world rapidly changing, yet this place has a sense of timelessness.

Atlantic Edge, inspired by the cliffs of Moher, brings to mind the opening words of Genesis: *In the beginning God created the heavens and the earth . . . and the Spirit of God was hovering over the waters.* These words are echoed in the first line of John's Gospel which speaks of Christ: *In the beginning was the Word, and the Word was with God, and the Word was God . . . Through him all things were made.*

God's creation or handiwork points to his goodness, beauty and truth, and Paul writes: *For we are God's workmanship, created in Christ Jesus to do good works, which God prepared in advance for us to do* (Eph 2:10). The Greek word here for handiwork or workmanship is *poiema*, from which we get the English word, poem. God, who is love, writes his poetry in countless ways on our lives, and gives us the task of doing the same for others.

2

October Moonlight

I thought I saw something deeper, more infinite, more eternal than an ocean—in the expression in the eyes of a baby.

—Vincent Van Gogh, letter to Theo, 10 December 1882

OCTOBER MOONLIGHT

In humid October moonlight
when a million chiming crickets
and a gamelan ensemble
played their symphonies
to the southern galaxies
a tiny form, your babe was born,
dark and beautiful like you—
Hartini, the woman we never knew.

In piercing November noon-light
where a crimson-leafed poinsettia tree
and a fruit-laden vine
sheltered home and garden
from the harsh sunshine
she took you from her heavy breast
and left with empty shawl
and wept.

She'd told of her sorrow at having to part,
how she hoped you'd do well and be clever;

The prayer that I offer, the pastor replied,
is for God's love to dwell in her heart.

I found you, wrapped you in my arms,
joy knows no bounds—it sets us free—
with light of sun and moon and stars
you filled my home and danced with me.

THE PLAYHOUSE WINDOW

Looking out at us
from the bamboo playhouse window
he, two, you, three
(remember the carpenter—
we paid him a visit in the tiny cabin
he built like this
on the edge of the river)
your eyes that sparkle like sun on water,
your faces, ripples of laughter,
warmth, the shine on your black hair,
duck-down blond of his.

We'd lose him
search for him everywhere
then through the window
find him asleep
with handfuls of half-eaten tangerines
in this snug retreat
armfuls, hugfuls of pillows.

With zest you'd set the scene for play,
choose props and hats,
give him his part in the story;
he'd follow a moment
then choose his own way
the plot you'd adapt
sketch new words to say.
In a flash—your childhood—
a snap of a day.

AFLAME

I hear the pitch of your scream
in the heat of the sun
running feet on the grass
see the flames on your hair
you race to my arms
I fly like the wind to yours
spread my circle of skirt
fling its blue cotton flowers all around you
smother the licks and forks of fire
stifle the singe of your long locks of hair
bathe the beautiful skin of your face—
soothe the scorch of fear—
in cold running water.

You were the space of a heartbeat
the flick of a hair
an angel's wing-width
a gust of air
a gasp, a snatch, a flare
a breath away
from disaster
the searing burn of flesh
that day as a child—
when I still could be near—
the first time
in a lust for wild adventure
you played with fire.

DRAGONFLY

The dragonfly dances
on dew-laden foliage
gossamer wings
iridescent in sun

Its sparkle entrances you
child of an early age
you glide and quiver
and chase it in fun

Its dazzle of color
you instantly capture
with dashes of paint
in your first picture

Now seventeen
you celebrate
with wings of gold thread
on the dress you have made

of shimmering fabric
a dawn pink shade
reflections of sunlight
to commemorate

the dragonfly
who can fascinate
a free spirit
in flight.

PASS IT ON

Markisa fruit, my parting gift—
I think that few have tasted
a fruit so sweet and succulent—
my harvest wasn't wasted;

you squeezed and sieved the juice,
it dripped like honey from your lips,
then on your garden compost tip
you threw away the pips.

I left the land and then came back,
my precious plant was gone,
the root was withered, leaving chaff
where luscious fruit had hung.

But then you brought your welcome gift,
fruit from your passion vine,
sprung from the ash heap where you'd flung
the seeds—your gift from mine.

CRUST OF THE EARTH

I hold a small round stone in my hand
lifted from a childhood pathway

magma, rough and pitted
spewed from the cone of Merapi

kindled in the core of our existence
held close to our heart, family.

LANTERNS

One small distant glow appearing,
pinpoint in the pitch-dark night
at the clang of the gong
on the wooden church door—

then dots, like fireflies emerging,
gleam after gleam
along the curve of the valley,
highlighting

shoulders, faces,
golden in lamplight,
feet on newly-lit pathway
tracing the contours of rice terraces.

Soon the building fills
with each lamp entering
and through windows and doors wide open
they shine, beacon-bright on the slopes,

with the luminescence
of stained glass in cathedrals—
the radiance,
living lanterns of witness.

REFLECTION

Living in community

It was in a big house overlooking Murlough Bay with a view of the Mourne Mountains that we first met, at a student retreat. Jim was doing research on William Blake's poetry at Edinburgh University at the time, and I was majoring in English and Religion as part of Education Studies in Belfast. We were at the conference because we believed this was a crucial time in our history, and that peace in our community was only possible if barriers of prejudice and resentment could be broken down. The starting point to restored relationships was recognizing God's love and forgiveness through Christ, getting to know more of the Holy Spirit's living presence in our lives, and seeking to be messengers of peace in whatever way he would lead us.

Sometime later, just as Jim and I were finishing our studies and about to take up teaching posts near Belfast, a friend who is a gifted Bible teacher and the speaker at the retreat, Roy Millar, contacted us individually. Roy was a busy plastic surgeon in the Burns Unit of the biggest hospital in Belfast throughout all the years of the troubles in Northern Ireland. He was moving with his wife Rosemary and two young children to a large terraced house in the nearby coastal town of Holywood, to form a community who would pray and serve in the local church and neighborhood. There was also a growing fellowship who gathered weekly in their home, young people who would later become the core of a large church serving the neighborhood of East Belfast. He asked if we would like to be part of their household and we both agreed, unaware how this decision would affect the course of our lives

During evenings spent chatting over books and papers as we did preparation for teaching, and through the routine tasks of living and relating to one another in community, we soon got to know each other. Jim and I realized that as students, before we ever met, we had both been following events in Indonesia and praying for the country, and were interested in going at some stage of our lives to work there.

After some months, as Jim and I grew closer and shared our feelings for one another, we knew we wanted to spend the rest of our lives together. We got married a year later and moved to a home of our own. Living as part of a family-based community had helped prepare us for the community-oriented home life that we would experience later in Indonesian culture, and the Millars were an example to us of servant leadership and openhearted hospitality. Our time spent relating as a group and in the local church resulted in close and lasting friendships that would be of enormous support to us through the years ahead, as we left all that was familiar and moved to distant places.

Jim and I had four more years gaining teaching experience in local schools and then after talking with our Presbyterian Church in Ireland about mission overseas and following various leads, we accepted the invitation sent by the Council of Churches in Indonesia to go and teach at Satya Wacana Christian University in Central Java. (Satya Wacana means "faithful to the Word"). We completed professional qualifications in teaching English as a foreign language and then began to study Indonesian at the Zendingshuis of the Netherlands Reformed Church near Leiden in Holland, while waiting for a visa.

Some Indonesian background

It had been a tumultuous time in Indonesia, and the Christian church was growing very fast. There were two main reasons for that. First, there were many new converts from a Christian revival that was happening in parts of the country, especially in the southeastern islands. Second was the aftermath of the failed Communist coup in 1965, in which hundreds of thousands of people died in conflict between the Muslim majority and the large number of Communist sympathizers.

The new government's answer was to ensure Indonesia firmly remained a religious state, and require everyone to follow one of five recognized religions. That left many people having to find a religion, and in the late 1960s, between two and three million people registered as Christians and joined the church. The development of Indonesian Christianity is a fascinating story and this sudden growth needs put in context. James Haire's review of Aritonang & Steenbrink (eds.), *A History of Christianity in Indonesia* (Leiden and Boston, MA: Brill, 2008), points to some key reasons for the growth of a strong indigenous church in Indonesia: Indonesians themselves spreading the faith to their own people and developing their own indigenous theologies, a firm nationalist tendency that united Christians with others (a unity that had begun during the Dutch colonial period, and continued into the independence struggle at the end of World War Two and thereafter in the independent nation), a strong focus on social justice, and the churches' role in nation building (ecommons.cornell.edu).

The aftermath of the failed Communist coup in 1965 was a time of great fear and insecurity throughout the country and for many people Christianity offered a new stability and confidence. The Christian focus on a battle between the kingdom of God and the forces of darkness in which Christ has already won the victory also resonated with many on hearing the gospel for the first time. The ultimate reason for growth was undoubtedly the work of God's Spirit in people's lives, fulfilling Christ's promise to build his church (*Indonesian Revival: Why Two Million Came to Christ*, Avery T. Willis, William Carey Library, 1977).

An appeal went out from the Council of Churches in Indonesia to partner churches around the world for support in teaching and caring for these new Christians. It was an exciting time, but there were obviously huge logistical challenges for the small under-resourced Christian community. The Dutch had left behind Christian schools when Indonesia won its battle for independence in 1949 (first proclaimed in 1945), and there was now a great need for support in the training of teachers for Christian schools, universities and theological colleges to meet the needs of the huge influx of new Christians.

The first two couples from our Presbyterian Church in Ireland who responded to the call for help were James and Mary Haire who went to the island of Halmahera, and Ken and Valerie Newell to Timor. It was James Haire's visits to our home church and his inspirational talks about Indonesia that first roused my interest as a student, and Ken Newell and his enthusiasm for all he had experienced in Indonesia rekindled Jim's interest.

Ken's book, *Captured by a Vision*, is an inspiring account of his courageous and untiring work for peace and reconciliation in Ireland alongside Catholic priest, Father Gerry Reynolds, a lifelong bridge-building commitment that had its roots in the Newells' time in Timor, Indonesia.

Moving to Indonesia

Convinced that this was a God-given opportunity for us to go and be involved, when our visas came through, we resigned from our jobs, left our families and friends, and faced the unknown with joy and anticipation.

Just before our departure, the others who'd been third-culture kids in my family also left home. My brother Jim, an engineer, went to the UAE where he met his future wife Kath, and later settled in Australia. My sister Eileen, just a year older than me, went back to her roots in Nigeria to teach RE in a school in Jos. There she met and married David Owers, and like Eileen herself, their children Kevin and Rebecca were born and brought up in Nigeria. Unable to go to Eileen's wedding, I celebrated by decorating every room in my new home in Java with flowers, like the red and yellow canna lilies we'd known in our childhood home.

It was a difficult time for our parents saying goodbye to three of their children within the space of a few months, and particularly for Rosemary the youngest, just starting Education and Music studies when we left. I missed them hugely too: in a world before emails and instant communication, Indonesia seemed the ends of the earth from Ireland. Years later when we were back in Ireland, Rosie and Jonny Irvine, also musically gifted, were married. Somehow all of us managed to be together in one place for that special celebration.

The biggest sorrow that clouded our own lives as we set out for Indonesia was that, unlike so many of our married friends who already had children, we seemed to be the exception. Despite all our hopes and prayers, there was continual disappointment. It's hard to overstate the grief couples go through in this situation. We inquired about adoption while in Ireland, but the waiting list was closed because of so few infants needing adopted.

Being childfree made the move to a completely new culture and climate less of an upheaval than it might have been and it gave us more time to adapt and learn the language on arrival. We found Java with its steep mountains and lush vegetation, bright tropical colors and markets with fruit in abundance, a truly beautiful place; its rich culture of batik art, gamelan music, puppet theater and dance drama, unique and fascinating. The friendliness and welcoming attitude of the Indonesian people was a joy. We soon got used to the new routine of boiling our drinking water, bathing by scooping cold water from a tank over us on to the floor, and making sure to cover up in the evening when the mosquitoes came out in force.

A new community

Starting teaching on campus helped us to get to know staff and students. We lived in the grounds of the halls of residence used by students from the outer Indonesian islands. Satya Wacana Christian University in the sprawling market town of Salatiga, was a wonderful example of ethnic diversity in a country with more than 300 distinctive ethnic groups, and 700 separate languages. The language chosen as the official language at independence in 1945 was Bahasa Indonesia, a variety of the Malay language long in use as the lingua-franca.

From the students' frequent visits to our home, we learned about the very different cultures of their individual islands. We shared homemade ice cream and cake and listened to their stories of families they had to leave behind, their struggles with finance and, long into the night, and at shower time early in the morning, we heard them singing or playing music in their dorms across the lawn. As our language skills increased, we held a regular home-study group for students, focusing on the Gospel of John. We had entered another kind of community lifestyle, and quickly felt at ease and privileged to be part of it. It wasn't long before we opened our home to students who needed somewhere to stay, like Aprini and Sunarsih, both from Java, Saarja from Timor and Tress from Ambon, each welcomed at different times as part of the family.

New arrival

Just six months after coming to our new home, I got a letter out of the blue from a friend Barbara to say that she'd had a dream that I was pregnant. She prayed about whether to tell me and then had the same dream again, so she wrote in faith that I'd soon have a child. She also had longed for children and some months later, adopted a baby daughter. Two weeks after her letter came, our life transforming event took place, taking us, and all our curious neighbors, by surprise. As soon as a line of freshly washed baby clothes suddenly appeared in our garden, students started calling to investigate.

Just a few days before, American colleagues who already had a grown-up family came to see us. They'd had a very unexpected visit from a man asking if they would adopt a baby born to a relative of his who'd come from Jakarta to give birth in the local hospital. Because of her circumstances, the baby's mother was unable to keep the child. We knew how rare this was, as children who needed care were usually provided for by the extended family, or given on loan to an orphanage so they could be claimed back when they were older.

We wanted to know more about the situation, so we went at once to Australian friends, Tony Nichols (who later became Bishop of North West Australia) and his wife Judith, both working in ministry in the university and the church in Indonesia. Their understanding of the local culture was an immense help to newcomers like ourselves. They arranged for the baby's mother to meet with a local colleague so they could talk to her directly in Javanese, her mother tongue, and see what she really needed and wanted to be done. She explained her situation and said that she would feel comforted if the family adopting her baby would love her and treat her as their own child, because sometimes children could be adopted by local families in order to be brought up as household servants.

So that is how the amazing gift in my poem *October Moonlight* came to be with us, just two weeks old, making us very aware of the opposite poles of sadness and joy that accompany every adoption.

When we knew she was coming to us, Jim and I made a shortlist of our favorite names, and decided on Suzanne. Then we discovered that on her birth certificate she was named Susanti, the Indonesian equivalent, and we were grateful for this personal sign to us of a loving God that had led us and this child together at the right time. Soon I was taking our new daughter everywhere with me in a brightly colored batik selendang, the shawl or sling used by local mothers to carry their babies close to them.

Intercountry adoption

Waiting for the formal process of adoption, we were faced with obstacles, not the least being permission from the UK Home Office for a foreign adoption. We knew time was limited because some fundamentalist groups were pressing for legislation to prevent foreign adoptions. After a year of repeatedly asking, the document came and the Indonesian court procedure followed successfully. I remember leaving the court with our baby, already taking her first steps by then, rejoicing with the assurance, *no one shall pluck them from my hand.* Like the image in those words of Jesus, a child was now secure in her parents' hands, to be loved and treasured always. Later I would grow to recognize more of how adoption is a picture of our relationship as children in God's family. Just a couple of weeks after the court hearing, the Indonesian government passed a law banning foreigners from adopting. Again we were greatly relieved that we had made it in time.

We had given a lot of thought to the difficulties that might be faced by a child in an interethnic adoption. Even before Suzanne began to show curiosity about skin color differences, the story of her birth mother, and how she as a baby came to be with us, was one we often related. We talked about how wonderful it is that each person is unique and how differences make us special. She often asked questions and we would give answers that we felt she was ready for.

Her most pressing question would be why her birth mummy wasn't able to look after her.

The biggest, most difficult questions about life are always the why questions, often about suffering and separation and relationships. Sometimes they can never be answered in words but only by being surrounded with unconditional love. I wanted to show my children that what happened with their original parents was not a reason for laying blame, and that when we live in the love of the family we have now, we are safe in that love. We are safe because of God's love; no matter what happens in our lives, we can always come to the Father. He accepts us entirely as we are; in his love no human being need feel any sense of rejection or unworthiness. These are truths that we ourselves as adoptive parents brought to mind at many stages of our lives.

From the Playhouse Window introduces our second child who came with us to Indonesia as a toddler soon after we adopted him in Ireland. His story is remarkable, and told in the next chapter.

Suzanne had the great advantage of growing up in her own ethnic culture before we had to move back to Ireland. We took our children at holiday times to see how people lived in other parts of the country, like Sumatra, Sulawesi and Bali. We watched batik artists at work in Yogyakarta and went to magnificent outdoor performances of classical Javanese and Balinese dancing. Suzanne enjoyed classes with local children to learn something of these skills herself and village children joined us for Bible stories, songs and crafts in our garden.

Our children grew up with a love for Indonesia, especially the food: the abundance of unusual tropical fruits and the tasty dishes using all the local spices. Suzanne still cooks many of these for her own family and is certainly blessed with artistic gifts that are part of her Indonesian heritage. It was our daughter's early interest in cooking that led to her attempt as a child to light a charcoal burner, while playing with a friend in the garden, resulting in the event in the poem *Aflame*.

From early childhood she was outgoing and friendly and enjoyed all the attention she got from the students, neighbors and other children at school. Complete strangers would stop us frequently to ask about our Indonesian child. The love and acceptance shown to both our children by Indonesians as well as their grandparents, extended family and friends in Ireland, helped them feel greatly valued.

In the villages

Our eleven years spent teaching English and Christian Education and bringing up our daughter and son in the sunshine as well as the tropical storms was a greatly enriching time in our lives. One special experience was being involved in the work of the church in the mountain villages outside the town where we lived, with weekly visits there to help the children and young people who were so keen to learn English.

The villages had small church buildings and we taught the children who would gather, using games, songs and Bible stories with pictures and mime which enabled them to start learning English. Kids whose families did not want them inside a church would stand and watch at the open doors and windows. The Indonesian pastor we worked with was a man of great energy and vision, and we were privileged to be part of his team at a time of exciting church growth in the villages of that region. *Lanterns* was written after visiting a weekly youth gathering held in one of these villages.

As well as Indonesians friends, especially the very dedicated staff at the university, we met wonderful people who'd come from many parts of the world, like American friends, Marilyn and her husband John who worked in theological education. Marilyn features in my poem *Pass It On*. All these committed people demonstrated how good it is to pass on what we've received to others.

3

Song in the Night

If something in you yourself says "you aren't a painter"—
it's then that you should paint . . . and that voice will be
silenced too.

—VINCENT VAN GOGH, LETTER TO THEO, 28 OCTOBER 1883

NESTLING

Baby, did you know
the scent of your mother,
the murmur of her voice
as you snuggled inside her?
Did you share her pangs of fear
while you nestled there?

And in the moment of your trauma
when the cord that bound you to her
wound around and choked you
did your mind record the struggle
as your heartbeat dipped and fluttered
like a little fallen bird?

Did you sense the panic
when the midwife seized you
and snipped the cord
your skin so very blue
and you didn't gasp
or utter any cry?

Resuscitated.
Ventilated.
You wrestled in a battle not to die.
Little babe, a lion cub
was not as brave as you.

And when she had to leave
did you miss her touch?
Did you feel lost, little lamb?
I wasn't there to hold you
babe, I didn't even know you.
You were settled in a foster mother's care—

then swept away.
Little child, how did you bear
another separation
when they brought you to us suddenly that day
with your grey, furry mouse
and your little blue jumper?

How did you ever learn
that you don't need to test our love,
that I am your forever mother,
that your father's love will keep you?
How do we learn
just to nestle and to trust?

ANESTHESIA

Wrapped in fibrous tissue
salt-crust of tears
the soul
layer on layer
unpeeling
onion skin of years

To the haunting notes of Enya
the mind floats adrift
Gaelic chants
echo through centuries
castles churn in island mists
gulls keen on lonely coasts

Light ebbs, the sky blurs
low-level clouds scud
a whole body sucked
by the relentless tide
numbly I succumb
to the wave-tug

Two figures, white-clad
appear on the horizon
come, steer me swiftly
through this
vast
chasm.

SLEEPLESS

Tonight my body aches too much
to hold you or be held
I listen to the motion of your breath
on the pillow, consistent pattern
whisper of waves on a distant ocean
this long December night of my silent wakefulness

and let the trusted rhythm enfold me
wrap me in garlands of scented silk
gift me with droplets of healing myrrh
incense
peace
pervading the darkness.

Starlight on the seas
on the fields
on the manger of my soul
love's presence
gift of gold
in the stillness.

Asleep or sleepless
in health or sickness
love lifts
and holds us
never lets go.

DREAM SHADOW

Eagle-winged, the oil lamp
sends its gleam
through chiseled leather puppets to a screen
creating shadow-beings in the night
mythic, other-worldly, like a dream
tales of Ramayana, conflict, flight.

But in my dream
the phantom shapes were crafted
from matted shreds, a filigree, blood-red
scarcely human, yet I knew them
nameless fragments, unformed children
circling and shadowing my bed.

In cold daylight I see their identity
children of Lir, excluded from humanity.
I hear the swan song
the long, last cry
nest robbed
hope nurtured, gone.

From eagle-lamp
to wild-swan-wing
have I travelled half a life
have I journeyed half a world
in the shadow of a dream
in the echo of a song?

SONG IN THE NIGHT

Enthralled by the power emanating
from the small woman in mid-life
dark-haired, olive-skinned, dressed in red
walking through the city streets
crowds followed as she led

unnerved, head held high, eyes fixed
as if on the invisible source
of her creative energy.

Children reached out their hands
as if to touch
a fountain of rainbow colors
vibrant with joy as she sang—
For I have new life within me
again and again.

The melody and aura of dream-sleep
awakened deep within me
fresh water streams.

Years later, on a night out
as if in another life
sitting with a friend in the Waterfront Hall
an orchestra playing
then on to the stage walks again
the soloist, petite brunette
dressed in vivid red
voice filling the auditorium.

Real-life mirror of a dream.
Dream-life relived in song.

HEALING SEASON

Fisherman's net cast, outspread, empty
Web spun tight on a window of sky
Vessels and nerves beneath the skin
        magnified, ramify
Lines defining generations
        marriages and procreations
Map of mazes, lanes and junctions
        intersections, terminations
Knots of fabric, ripped and ragged
Barbed wire fences, stark and jagged
Shards and splinters, mesh on cages
Scalpel scar on flesh and pages—
The stripped and desolate branches
        I trace their intricate patterns—
This dark winter's trees.

A bud unseals
        the fist-grip loosens
Leaf-hand uncurls
        translucent in the sun
Bud scales unpeel
Blossoms swell and open, sheen of moonlight
        cream and blue and white and silver pearls.

On a branch in the warmth of a woven nest
        embryo life is throbbing
        wings wet, crouched and waiting
        for the shell-crack-opening—
Entry to a world transformed
        those dreary trees now adorned—
Mystery, this jewelry of Spring.

REFLECTION

A two-week window of opportunity

The circumstances surrounding the arrival of our second child were to us quite miraculous. I'd made a short trip back to Northern Ireland to introduce Suzanne to our family, after her Indonesian adoption and a visa to enter the UK on my passport had been granted. During the few weeks I was there, the adoption waiting list that had been closed for years was re-opened for just two weeks.

I rang to inquire and was told that the expected number of applications during those two weeks would take the next two years to process. Whoever applied now would be selected at random to begin interviews, and we would have to be available for these in Ireland, wait for a child to be available, and then go through the courts. So I put our name down and returned to Indonesia knowing that in human terms, to adopt within their time schedule and keep our visa for Indonesia from expiring, was highly improbable.

A surprise letter

Then a few weeks later in July, we got a letter: we had been selected randomly as the first couple to start interviews. We replied that the earliest we could leave Indonesia was the following February when we were due to renew our visa. That would allow us to spend up to a year back in Ireland. Social Services told us that we would have to decide between Indonesia and adoption as there was no likelihood of getting everything through within the time we suggested. We asked them to keep us on the list and we would be glad to start in February. As with everything, we prayed.

When we got back to the UK, it turned out that an apparently inflexible system was prepared to make special arrangements for us. A social worker was scheduled to speed things up by doubling the interviews in a shorter time frame, the first being held in the home of our close friends, Roy and Rosemary Millar, where we stayed for a week or two before getting into our own house. After months of rigorous questioning, we were approved, and told we would hear if a child was ready to be placed with us.

An extraordinary combination of circumstances

In August we went for a week to stay in the Millars' caravan in Donegal. It rained constantly, so we decided to come back a couple of days early. The Millars asked us to drop off a bag at their house on the way home so we went there first. We had just opened the door with their key when the house phone rang. It was a social worker wanting to speak to us. A boy of 13 months was available for adoption and could we take him as soon as possible? She would bring him to see us the next day as the foster mother had to go away for some time.

I was astonished. Why did she use this house phone number? This was the number on her records, she told me. We had been at that address for only about a week several months ago, I told her. If we hadn't happened to call for two minutes at our friends' house, what would they have done with the child? It was very urgent, she replied, so she would've phoned the next couple on her list.

The rain in Donegal that brought us home several days early, the bag that needed dropped off, the phone number of a house where we'd spent just a week or two some months before, the phone call at the precise moment we arrived after a 120 mile drive from Donegal, not intending to be more than two minutes in the house; all these circumstances coming together we saw as evidence of divine providence, an encouragement through the years that all was in God's plan from the very beginning.

Nestling is about our son. Within a few days, after a short 'getting to know you' visit, little Paul with blond curls and blue eyes arrived together with a brief family history, referring to his birth trauma and a reference to the challenges he would face. The court proceedings were arranged for some months later.

The first challenge was helping him adapt to a new family situation. He immediately saw in Suzanne a potential best playmate and his way of trying to connect with her consisted of getting hold of anything she played with. He soon began to walk and his first words every day were go, go, go, but outside he objected to being fastened in a buggy and preferred to be the one pushing it. He always wanted to run rather than walk and to be independent rather than holding anyone's hand.

The judge at the family court was patient as Paul literally ran rings around his table, which was preferable to having him struggle on our knee. Two adoptions were successfully completed, (Suzanne had to have a UK adoption as well), our house cleaned and rented out again, and four suitcases packed with supplies for our growing family, just before we had to say goodbye once more to our very supportive family and friends, and board a plane to return to Indonesia in time to renew our visa. Once again everything had fitted in just before the deadline.

The outdoor life in the sunny climate of Indonesia was good for a very active toddler, even though he needed constant supervision as our garden area opened on to the student hostel grounds and Paul loved it when students would stop on their motor bikes and take him for a ride. Once when we were at an Indonesian colleague's house for a meal, we thought he was safe with other children in their fenced back garden. Suddenly the host stopped eating and ran outside. In the far corner of the garden, Paul was standing on the ledge of an open well staring down. He was hastily grabbed to safety by our host and we've never enjoyed a meal with more relief.

As a child he was at his happiest and easiest to entertain when in the swimming pool, never listening to instructions but learning to swim aged five by jumping in the deep end and splashing his way to the other side as I watched him. After some years at school, it was evident that he needed the support available in the UK, and our daughter would have to prepare for transfer to secondary level. We were already more than ten years in Indonesia and were told this was the maximum time allowed for foreign work permit extensions, so we sadly said goodbye to our many friends and the place we loved, sorted our belongings and headed back to County Down. We were very blessed because shortly after our return to Ireland, a rare job came up at the university as a lecturer in English to trainee teachers, which Jim applied for and got.

Autistic spectrum challenges

Our experience in the years that followed has shown us that young people on the autistic spectrum live in a world little understood by others. Impulsive speech and behavior, and difficulties such as connecting cause and consequence, learning from mistakes and moderating conduct according to social norms, mean that they easily become the objects of blame and the targets of bullying. They long for acceptance yet continually have to cope with rejection.

The challenges of teenage years are magnified for young people with ASD and their families. The absence of reliable, stable friendships and of welcoming social groups in the community makes it a very vulnerable time, when issues of frustration, low self-esteem and self-harm become especially frequent. Seeking to regain control, demand avoidance behavior becomes the norm. Parents are involved in their child's difficulties on an ongoing basis, repeatedly trying to find the trigger and solution for every problem before it multiplies in its effects.

A lack of opportunity for a child with this condition to be accepted among young people at church made us realize how important it is for churches to be more aware and make welcoming spaces that are autism-friendly. Added to this was the general lack of understanding, mentoring or learning support provision at secondary school level at that time, despite our frequent visits and letters.

Unlike many, Jim and I had each other's support, even though we felt the strain on our resources and our times alone together were often taken up with having to talk and struggle through every issue that arose.

I am able to empathize with a BBC news report I have just read about a family with an autistic child: "they were driven out of their home as a result of bullying, abuse and physical assault. The authorities failed to help them, they say, and mistook the symptoms of autism for aggression and unwillingness to cooperate . . . The abuse culminated in an attack on the couple's eldest son who has Tourette's syndrome and autism . . . After the assault . . . he was punching doors and walls and cutting his hands open, just pure frustration." Increasing awareness and understanding are starting points to making communities and churches more inclusive, and life for families a little more bearable.

The God who holds on to us

Our daughter had her own teen issues, and at the same time Jim was trying to keep control of type one diabetes that had been diagnosed in Indonesia, and I was suffering acute anemia, and eventually had to have surgery. There were days when we felt we didn't know where to turn for support, and the only prayer we could utter was a cry for help.

We believe in a loving, caring God who never ceases involvement in our challenges and he gave us hope at each point of despair. We were blessed by caring family, especially our sisters Janet and Rosie, always ready to listen and give support when they could, and some friends who knew of our heartaches and prayed with us, giving us encouragement and strength for the next crisis. We knew that as we navigated our way through it, we would gain insights of a kind that no other experience would have brought us. Someday, perhaps, we could be a support to people in similar deep waters, for we knew there was a world out there with families facing hugely challenging situations, and long waiting-lists for young people with anxiety issues.

With young adults, ultimately you have to let them make their own choices, even though we know the consequences might be difficult. When we entrust them to God's hands, and always stick by them, we can believe that the path they choose might be long and rough, but it is God who holds on to them.

Adoptive parents can take heart from the words of the chief executive of Adoption UK, Sue Armstrong Brown, who points out that, although adopted children often come from complex situations, leaving them vulnerable, "adoption can have a transformative effect on these children, and the testimony of adoptive parents is proof that you can successfully parent children . . . if the right support is in place."

Illness and steps to recovery

Song in the Night and other poems were written shortly after surgery one winter. Recuperation was an opportunity to reflect on and verbalize emotions that re-emerged at the time, partly through dreams (as in two of the poems), the kind of dreams that let you look into the pool of your own thoughts, or let you experience another way of hearing some hidden voice of wisdom, which can be God's way of speaking to us.

I learned to reassess recurring, apparently negative images in dreams, like the ravine that sometimes appears abruptly on my pathway and I have to begin the descent by ladder or steps, or find footholds in the clefts of the cliff. I interpret this image no longer as one of fear or anxiety, but one of faith, the faith to go downwards into the darkness, often to find someone that you care for there, and then go forward taking them with you. I've learned that the cliff edge in my dreams, often expressing the events in life that are unfathomable, is the abyss of faith.

4

Touch Down

I feel there's nothing more genuinely artistic
than to love people.

—Vincent Van Gogh, letter to Theo, 18 September 1888

TOUCH DOWN, SUMBA ISLAND

Indian
Ocean
lapis lazuli
ultramarine
foam-stitched
rock-studded
pearl-white-spattered
dappled with jasper-black
like a curtain unfolding
unveiling a coastline, sand,
a ribbon of gold, edged the parched land like an embroidered
vintage map unrolled, hills, bleached and tanned, deep indigo
valleys with the silver gleam of a single thread of stream,
glint of square sequins, roofs of tin,
on a woven fabric of stubble,
palms and stone, motifs
of cattle and horses
as we descended
in our giant
dove shadow
and
landed.

YOUR NAME RINGS OUT (at the church in Lambanapu)

Lambanapu,
your name rings out
like the rhythm of the gongs and drums
that welcomed us,
that guided the swift feet of the dancers,
their leaps and twirls,
their waving shields and swords,

children, barefoot,
beating time to your tune
in cloths intricately woven by mothers,
bodies gracefully synchronized
in lines and circles,
then one by one sat down.

Esther,
your name rings out
from the stones of that building,
lead dancer, Sunday school teacher,
your voice cries out
through the arid hills
as your beautiful feet

tread the rough paths
where villages are scattered,
climbing slopes to homes
where children are gathered
to listen to good news you bring
and step to the rhythm
of your life-giving song.

Esther pleased the king
and won his favor
and was made queen.

Your story
that you shared with me
with shining eyes
has its own place in history

and he walks with his chosen bride
through dust and thorns and rubble
to reach and hold and cradle
the smallest child.

LOVE FEAST (at Rajaka)

Magenta cloak of bougainvillea
enveloped the veranda
of the bamboo house.

As if entering the tree itself
we stepped into the world
which was their home,

unfurnished, except a simple table
prepared for us, steamed rice,
goat soup, spiced vegetable.

We savored the love feast
and entered the life,
the heart of goodness,
of husband and wife.

FISHERMAN AND HIS CHILDREN

As if carved from ebony
he stands, his mantle draped
on the bend of his shoulder.
Leaning on a knotted stick
he surveys us silently;
only his jaw moves,
mouth stained blood-red
chewing betel.

Behind him, three generations
in one room—the ancestral home
perched on a platform of bamboo
on stilts anchored deep in the earth,
the peaked roof-thatch,
tall as the village megalith,
storing bones, heirlooms,
objects of ritual.

Beneath the floor, piglets snuffle,
chickens peck and scrape.
On the bamboo steps a young mother
suckles her baby, her fifth she tells us.
Children in tattered tee-shirts cluster,
one flutters up a tree
for a bird's-eye view
of our arrival.

Beyond are the sandy beaches
and turquoise sea—
childhood playground
and place of toil and trial;
the fisherman
and his children's children
crafting together
for survival.

THE MANGER AND THE COW

It used to be a tree,
branches arching to the blue sky,
roots reaching
to gather moisture.

It used to be a dug-out canoe,
curved bark floating on the water,
children paddling with their father,
casting their lines.

Now it's a manger
where a bony white cow is tethered;
the wood is weathered and cracked
but it cradles the hay.

It used to be a calf,
a loan from God's people.
Now, fully grown,
it will soon be sold

to buy two calves—
for keeping, for giving—
some more seeds
for planting trees

and tackle for the fisherman
afloat with his children
who come to the boat
from the cradle.

THE PURSE (at Lewa skills training center)

I came here to learn to weave and sew
to share these skills for others to know;
my sister and friend from another shore,
here's my empty purse, I can't give more—

I spun the thread, dyed it, wove it,
shaped it, stitched it
before I ever met you
to make it your own special gift.
Take it, fill it, use it.

Her eyes spoke to me as she pressed
a portion of her life
into my empty hands.

LET ALL THE EARTH SING (a psalm at Lakoka)

Praise the Lord, all nations,
Let the whole earth sing

The sun falls like a ripe mango
behind the hills
and grass vibrates
with a chorus of crickets,
fronds of a coconut palm
wave as the earth cools,
song of a sunbird
from among banana leaves.

The white shell of a church
stands high on the hillside.
Within its frail walls
on a rubble floor and rough benches
is the life it nurtures—

people of all ages
from hills and farms and villages
on foot or riding horses,
join with all of nature
in one voice to sing:

Praise the Lord, all living creatures,
Give thanks to God our King.

FABRIC OF LIFE (Sumba ikat)

The cloth is a wedding gift to the groom,
emblem of the wealth and dexterity
of the bride's family,
in exchange for the bride price:
as many buffaloes and horses
as he can afford.

Each yarn, spun from plucked cotton,
counted and measured,
stretched on the warp and tied
with palm fibers
and dipped in dyes
of red kombu, turmeric, indigo—

bark, roots and leaves—
staining the hands
of girls and grandmothers,
guardians of messages
from the earth and ancestors—

intricate artistry—
turtles and crocodiles,
leaping horses,
shell-shedding lobsters,
symbols of lineage, royalty, rebirth.

Each cloth displaying
the threads of life,
gift at burial,
homage in death.

Mary and Martha,
a sister-fellowship,

the cloth,
your Sandalwood Island gift to us,
warp and weft—
your prayer and craftsmanship,

Terima kasih,
our deepest gratitude,
love received—
fabric of grace.

REFLECTION

South-eastern islands: Sumba and Timor

Sumba, formerly called Sandalwood Island, is part of a distinct archipelago of 246 inhabited islands in the south-east of Indonesia. This area is like a microcosm of the whole Indonesian archipelago which consists of 13,677 inhabited islands. The isolation between one island and another has led to a wide variety of separate cultures and arts. Sumba has one of the last surviving megalithic cultures in the world. Huge blocks of stone up to twenty tons in weight are cut and dragged great distances to construct tombs, traditionally in the center of each village, and preparations for a funeral can take up to a year.

Some years after our time living in Indonesia, we were asked to go back with an all-age team to establish a partnership between our Presbyterian Church in Ireland and the Sumba Christian Church.

The church in Sumba must be one of the fastest growing in the world. From around 6,000 members at the time of independence, proclaimed in 1945, it now has well over half a million members, a large majority of the island's population. The cultural practices of the traditional animistic religion called Merapu are still strong, but like many ancient, traditional cultures, Sumba is facing the influences of increasing modernity. With the fast growth of Christianity on the island, the church faces the challenge of how to contextualize the gospel in their own situation. Such a contextualization raises questions and looks for answers that only the people of Sumba themselves, led by God's Spirit, can provide, and importing a westernized form of Christianity will never deal with these issues.

As Alan Tippett explains in his book, *Introduction to Missiology* (Pasadena, CA, 1987), a church can be seen as indigenous when Jesus is no longer seen as a foreign import, when worship is offered in culturally understood ways, when their church structures fit the culture of their people, and when the cultural needs of their own community are being met.

We were also there to visit our partner church in Timor. The Christian University of Artha Wacana in Kupang already had a long-standing link with us through our church's mission workers, the Newells, and the Hannas teaching in the theology faculty. We also wanted to revisit Salatiga, the university town in Central Java where we'd previously worked, and meet with staff and student groups. It was good also to have a few days recreation in Bali, so we included a visit there at the end of the trip.

The poem *Touch Down* is our arrival in Sumba. The other poems give pictures of people we met there, those in traditional villages and inspirational Christian leaders, as well as some of the projects they had set up to help the local economy. Sumba, in the dry eastern part of Indonesia, was often overlooked by the central government in Jakarta, and suffered from unemployment and poverty, issues that the fast-growing church is trying to address. As we talked with various congregations all over the island, we were amazed to see how ministers coped, sometimes one pastor for as many as forty individual churches, and many of these groups had very few Bibles. Often these churches in the hills were accessible only on horseback.

Fabric of Life refers to the ikat cloth unique to Sumba, made with the most ancient of the world's weaving techniques, thought to have originated nearly 3000 years ago. The process can take up to a year for one cloth to be completed. The cloths, worn as garments on special occasions, are central to community life, used as gifts in ceremonial exchanges and especially at elaborate burial rituals with feasting. Each village and family has its own inherited motifs used in the design, and the pattern is memorized and passed on through generations. During our decade in Java, as a new semester approached, students from Sumba often called at our home with these precious cloths given to them by their families to exchange for university fees, so we acquired quite a few. The poem refers to a fellowship of Christian women in Sumba who call their organization Mary and Martha, identifying with the two sisters at Bethany who gave hospitality to Jesus, Martha who prepared the food and served, and Mary who spent time with Jesus listening to him as he taught.

The Purse relates to a girl I met at the Skills Training Centre at Lewa, set up by the church in Sumba. The aims of this place include protecting and promoting the island's traditional crafts, especially the skill of weaving, in order to boost the island's economy.

The money raised by our team on our return helped to rebuild and equip the center.

In every church community we visited in Sumba and Timor, we met leaders who had studied at Satya Wacana Christian University in Java and it was a great opportunity to renew friendships from our time teaching there. It is a real tribute to the values and standard of education at the university that it has produced so many men and women in leadership roles in church and state.

Shortly after the partnership was set up with Sumba, Mervyn McCullagh from Dublin was sent by our church in Ireland to work with the church there. After some time, he met and married Raing, a daughter of one of the traditional Sumbanese kings. Mervyn and Raing's website, (http://www.homeinsumba.com/about/info.htm), is not just an excellent source of information about Sumba, but also shares their considerable expertise on all aspects of Sumbanese culture and particularly ikat weaving.

Christian witness in Japan

Another touch-down event in our lives was arriving at Osaka Airport in Japan to teach at the Christian University of Kwansei Gakuin in Nishinomiya, near Osaka. It was a fascinating introduction to the work of the Christian church in the center of Honshu in Japan. We had the opportunity to be part of the work of a thriving Christian university with around 14,000 students at the time, (it has since doubled in size), and also to visit local churches and see something of their work.

Kwansei Gakuin has an impressive mission statement: "to be a learning community based on the principles of Christianity which inspires its members to seek their life missions, and cultivates them to be creative and capable world citizens who embody its motto, Mastery for Service, by transforming society with compassion and integrity."

Christianity is very much a minority religion in Japan, but it works hard not to be seen as a foreign, western import. We saw compassionate awareness of the challenges faced by young Japanese

Christians. Japanese religion puts more emphasis on cultural and social practices than on a system of beliefs. Ancestral rites are considered an essential part of life both to ensure the wellbeing of ancestors and also to promote the family's worldly success and prosperity.

We saw understanding for young Christians who struggle with the expected obligations of ancestor veneration in both the Shinto religion and Japanese Buddhism, and don't want to let down their grandparents who want the necessary rituals to see them into the afterlife. Churches sought to find ways of showing that they respect those who have gone before with memorial services for the dead.

The church seeks to use opportunities afforded by the huge demand for Christian weddings. Japanese people in general tend towards pluralism in their practices. "Born Shinto, marry Christian, die Buddhist" refers to the practices and rites that dominate birth, marriage and death.

We were also impressed to see the commitment of Japanese Christians in applying their faith to their lifestyles. For some, this meant refusing to impose on their school-age children long hours of cram school as soon as normal school was over and often at weekends. As Japanese people are very keen to learn English, we found churches active in providing free English classes for the community, and one church we visited had produced booklets of dramatized Bible stories with English language teaching points included.

The Christian church is small but a living, growing force in Japanese society and it was an exciting experience to be part of this during our time at the Christian university. Ian Miller's study *Choosing the Other: Conversion to Christianity in Japan*, (University of Manchester, 2010) provides a very good introduction to the growth of the Japanese church.

The Mango Tree Church

The Balinese Christian Church made a conscious decision nearly 50 years ago to use Balinese culture to express their faith, "sharing the water of life in a Balinese cup" as Bishop I Wayan Mastra put it. Buildings open to the air with streams of water running through, with small waterfalls, plants and flowers in abundance, beautiful Balinese carvings, and Balinese dancing to tell Bible stories, are all part of what Mastra called "the mango tree church." This is an apt symbol as the mango tree is evergreen, providing shelter in the heat and bearing fruit year after year. Neglected groups are a special focus of the church in Bali, with projects designed to help the disabled and those who live in impoverished communities.

It was a delight to drop into a church service in Denpasar, the capital city of Bali, one Sunday morning and discover part of the service was a wedding of two young Balinese couples, and the service started with a ceremony of baptism for all four of them. All of us in the congregation were invited to stay for a baptism-wedding celebration meal afterwards.

Mission is cross-shaped

I've referred to a growing Christian church in Indonesia, but when we talk about church growth, there's always a danger of falling into a market-based success model, where effectiveness is measured by the numbers who join. The only model we have been given to follow is that of Jesus himself, and that model is cross-shaped. It shows itself in sacrificial service out of love for and commitment to those on the outside.

When Peter expressed his faith in Jesus as the Son of God, Jesus promised that he would build his church on this rock. Then he told the disciples that he would be killed in Jerusalem but would rise again. When Peter immediately objected, Jesus rebuked him sternly and said, *If anyone would come after me, he must deny himself and take up his cross and follow me. For whoever wants to save his life will lose it, but whoever loses his life for me will find it* (Matt 16:24–25). Here we have the promise of Jesus that every sacrificial choice that is made in following him is life-giving.

As Paul writes: *We always carry around in our body the death of Jesus, so that the life of Jesus may also be revealed in our body . . . So then, death is at work in us, but life is at work in you* (2 Cor 4:10–12). At its best, the church in Asia has much to teach us about this, and it needs to be remembered that the church in many Asian countries knows what it is to suffer, facing shockingly high levels of persecution.

In our experience of Asian Christian communities, they showed in practical ways how the gospel must be demonstrated as well as proclaimed. Serving by setting up projects to improve the well-being and the economy of communities, rural and urban, has been an integral part of sharing the good news.

Cultural understanding

It is important for students in church leadership training in western countries to have opportunities for placements in cross-cultural settings. Learning to approach theology from another cultural stance helps us to identify which of our own beliefs or attitudes are molded by our home culture, rather than centered on the grace and truth of Christ. This helps us to build bridges, work as partners with people from different backgrounds and be peacemakers. This is very important in a polarized society like Northern Ireland where I live.

As followers of Jesus throughout the world, while we all share a Christ-centered identity and worldview, we can celebrate the fact that we have many cultural differences. In an increasingly globalized world, it is important that churches continue to value those aspects of the local culture that demonstrate the beauty and diversity of God's creation. We can also seek to uphold those who suffer where the prevailing culture is in opposition to faith in Christ.

Living among different cultures has given me the opportunity to enjoy the rich fabric with many threads and motifs, that is our human race. When we returned to Ireland, I continued teaching English as a foreign language, this time in a large Belfast school, Methodist College, which had a boarding department, and over the years I taught pupils from 30 different nationalities. Since retiring, I've been supporting the language learning of newcomers who arrive in our town from different parts of the world, people who really value our friendship. To be part of the international community here, and in the various countries where I've lived, is one of the greatest privileges life has given me.

5

Time Voyage

The heart of man is very much like the sea,
it has its storms, its tides and its depths;
it has its pearls too.
—Vincent van Gogh, letter to Theo, 31 October 1876

AT THE CRACK OF DAWN

Air, visible this morning,
tint, essence, zest
of lemon, citrus, lime,
a Pissarro pursuit,
a Turner bequest—
pulsating light.

Sunburst, audible
as chime bell, flute
awakening trees,
bird soprano,
poised wings,
flight.

Breeze, tangible,
stirring leaves,
the stroke of bow on strings,
light-fingering on keys
of a piano
at the behest of Chopin or Vivaldi.

You spoke at the beginning,
your voice still rings,
lights galaxies in space
and sparks each living cell,
a gallery of art,
an orchestra of grace.

BREATH-TAKING

Small, damp, dark
disk of the head
gradually emerging

to the rhythmic drumbeat
heartbeat of hope,

then a gasp, a blow,
a trumpet blast

and a whole new being
legs kicking

skates exuberantly
into the glare of day

first gulp of air
burst of a cry
waving of tiny hands.

Hey!
you're the miracle of life
beyond the scope
of all our dreams and plans
breathtaking treasure
we never thought to gain

jewel of sunlight
beams through the storm clouds
clear air
diamond fresh
after the rain.

TIME VOYAGE

1.

Soon after the split-half of the century
not far from the split-half of the globe
I slipped into existence, middle child of my family
voyaging between two continents,
from forests of palms on the vast River Niger
to Botanic Garden rose beds
near Grandpa's Belfast home;
roses—like beacons through the grey drizzle,
lamplights in grey streets, grey slates,
grey chimney smoke, all the warmth inside—
milk chocolate, Granny's apple pie, the blazing coal.

Back in the shade of our mission house veranda—
our school space, screened, mosquito-proofed—
we watched the changing colors of a chameleon,
a ripening mango, the fanlike wings of a butterfly
creeping from a chrysalis, the leaping and skipping
of children playing in the sun-scorched compound
in the brief interlude
between preparations for independence,
flags and drums, dances, celebrations,
and the savage slaughter of Biafran innocents.

I follow again the fire-flies' gleam in the humid half-darkness;
from the deck of the ocean liner
I watch the porpoises play.

A tree was axed I see a dugout drifting,
the boat upturned, the paddle lost, the rider missing.

2.

At the in-between age,
uprooted and transplanted,
I was educated (and segregated)
in the ancient capital with two cathedrals—
tower and spires, St Patrick duplicated
on twin hill tops in the orchard county;
reared in bog land, 'bandit country'—
sheep land where the air shimmers
and spring water cascades in ice-cold streams.
Ulster Blackwater straddles the border
that splits our island—and our family tree on either side.

We crossed the hills and heath by bus to school—
the walls, the gates, the avenue of cherries
where girls in green, selected and secluded,
the golden harp our badge, serenely gathered.
To books and boutiques, we were equally loyal,
to the Beatles, the Seekers and boys of the Royal
in the brief interlude
before the explosive history of our locality
was re-ignited as a daily reality
demolishing the myth of a civilized society.

I follow again the fire and the drums in the chilling half-darkness,
the tribal dance, the rattle of guns
while children play.

A ship at sea is lost, without a compass;
the harbor searchlight beams across the bay.

A LETTER COMES TO LIGHT

My very own dear . . . and then my name
you wrote the summer I was ten
before the winter of the big freeze
stopped your heart and lungs
like the wings of birds
that dropped from the sky
and wildlife drowned
in lakes trapped in ice,
and you were gone,

vanished
like the view of the hills and trees
when thick frost
blanked out our windows
and Arctic gales
blew snow in drifts
that blocked our doors.

My very own dear . . . in words penned to me
you appear
through the fog of half a century
that has passed between us
and your grandchild
is your age,
this letter has twinned us.

I finger the sketches you made,
jokes scribbled
on a faded blue page,
hear your voice, see you smile—
you'd the soul of a child—
as if here only yesterday,
one space back in a diary.

Your words like the sun,
like a warm blanket
bless me
like the greeting passed down
from the apostle of love
in the book you caressed
as you thumbed the worn pages:

My dearly loved children,
(he writes for all ages)
From the very first day
we have looked and seen,
our hands have touched,
our ears have heard,
From the beginning there's always been
Word of life,
Light of love.

WINDOW

You are the canvas
on which the colors of the landscape
first found shape
You are the frame
that lets the picture speak

You built the window
that lets the spectrum of the sunlight in
and when lights go out
and night comes in
I see the colors of the stars.

FOR THE NEXT LAP

First day, first leaf of October,
golden,
laden
with opportunity.

Green, copper and bronze
the trees of the glen
slope on the skyline
above roofs and eaves
right down to the shore.
Few days left at fifteen.

In a garden opposite
a tree spreads its branches
laden with apples,
little lanterns full of sunlight,
another cycle of nature
almost complete

and at night
if you look you will see
through the dark
far out on the headland
a lighthouse
flashing persistently.

Another year has elapsed,
this, the room
where your mother carried you
soon after birth
that cool autumn morning,
same view from this window

except that each year
trees grow imperceptibly,
like the world turning
unnoticeably
beneath our feet,
to bring a new day.

And as your world
begins another lap
around the sun
bringing unexpected challenges,
in these, the growing moments,
may you find

deep roots, hidden truths,
enduring connections;
and as new shoots spring up,
each unique leaf opens
and fruit ripens,
in time

with belief and nurture,
each dream, each chosen goal—
views far and near from a window—
will become the world
you help to shape
and enter.

VERY SPECIAL GEMSTONE

Millions of years ago
when continents collided
and rare elements coincided,
the lustrous ruby
had its birth,

secretly forming,
fiery and magical,
its magnificence hidden
in layers of rock
folding under the earth.

People who dug deep found it,
saw it glowing like the sun
as if a fire
burned from within,
giving healing powers.

Kublai Khan of China wanted it
in exchange for an entire city
and from Burma and Sri Lanka
the jewels came,
guarded in camels' loads,
riding the Silk highway,

welcomed at the gates of palaces
for kings to embellish
their armor and harnesses,
and in Bible times
worn on priestly garments,
the red precious stone of Reuben.

And in the Bible, we're told
in the age to come
the city of gold
with the radiance of rubies,
diamonds and sapphires
will fill the earth with heaven.

Experts search
for silk-needle inclusions
that shimmer like points
of a six-rayed star,
rare and dazzling
in the blood-red core—

Ruby, gift of love, a treasure
guarded, not on camelback
or on a sparkling horse,
cherished simply as you are,
queen of gems
the kindest friend

and when you smile
a star lights up
and glows in all our hearts.

REFLECTION

A new kind of family

I see myself as linking hands in a line of five generations whose lifetimes together span well over a century, people I have known and journeyed with: parents and maternal grandparents behind me, and in front, our son and daughter and grandchildren, joined to our family line by adoption. But relatives are not our only family. We've been enriched by being part of the family of God that spans the globe. In Christian communities in different places that have been our home, no matter what ethnic group we belong to, or denominational affiliation we may have, we are one family, *all sons of God through faith . . . all one in Christ Jesus* (Gal 3:26–28).

The New Testament uses two images to illustrate what it is to enter God's family. One is the picture of new birth, brought about by the life of God's Spirit, as described by Jesus (John 3:3–8). The second is adoption. Paul writes that God sent his Son so that we might receive adoption as sons and be heirs to God's promises (Gal 4:4–7). Paul uses the legal term meaning adoption to sonship, referring to the full legal rights of an adopted male heir in Roman culture.

Jesus didn't so much challenge our concept of family as blow it wide open and completely redefine it. There's something infinitely stronger than shared DNA and that's the love of God poured into our lives. When people from the crowd commented to Jesus about his family members, his reply showed that they were completely underestimating life in the kingdom of God.

Someone told him, "Your mother and brothers are standing outside, wanting to speak to you." He replied to him, "Who is my mother, and who are my brothers?" Pointing to his disciples, he said, "Here are my mother and my brothers. For whoever does the will of my Father in heaven is my brother and sister and mother" (Matt 12:46–50). And on another occasion when someone called out that his mother was blessed, he said, *Blessed rather are those who hear the word of God and obey it* (Luke 11:28).

That takes nothing away from the love within a biological or adoptive family. Jesus's care for his mother on the cross at the height of his suffering is astonishing: *When Jesus saw his mother there, and the disciple whom he loved standing nearby, he said to his mother, "Dear woman, here is your son," and to the disciple, "Here is your mother." From that time on, this disciple took her into his home* (John 19:26–27).

Through these words spoken to his mother and John at the cross, Jesus was signaling the new family of God, showing the model for relationships, taking care of one another, especially those who suffer loss, or are going through difficult times. For many who are isolated, perhaps because of family rejection, separation or death, or because of displacement from their home country or familiar neighborhood, the Christian family might be their only source of supportive, loving relationships. All relationships can be enriched, and especially those with whom we spend our lives in the closest natural relationship, if we are open to experiencing and sharing the love of God.

Awakening the past

At the Crack of Dawn began as lines I wrote long ago in a notebook when an art student friend and I spent some mornings outdoors "gathering poetry." We wanted to cross sensory boundaries and see air as color, smell and taste, and hear the light of dawn as sound, especially the music of birds. I think of the variety of nature and creativity as a constant reminder to us of the divine power that sparked a whole universe into existence. Each of us, made in his image, has creative potential and the ability to ignite creativity in others.

When I found my grandpa's letter, described in *A Letter Comes to Light*, it connected me with an inner child, one who had walked with my grandfather through city parks and in the countryside where we lived, as he listened to and mimicked birdsong and spotted wildflowers. He loved to go with us to an old schoolhouse covered in brambles and ivy, telling us stories about the ghosts of school children and the stern schoolmaster, and I guessed he was reliving his own childhood.

Grandpa loved to play the shiny, rose-wood piano which he had bought for my mum when she was a child, his rich tenor voice singing hymns or lively folk songs. He would show us the tiny space beneath the stairs in the house where they'd lived since the war and tell us stories of the blitz, the family huddling, squashed up under the stairs, hoping this would act as an air-raid shelter, and of his job through the blackout in the Second World War, driving important officials to secret destinations.

Granny was a gentle, brown-eyed woman. I think of their unspoken loss of so many babies, before and after birth, and wonder at their sacrifice after the war when their only child, my mother, a young single woman at the time, left to work in West Africa. When in her sixties she lost grandpa, James Spence, granny visibly lost part of herself as she'd always depended on him to make decisions and take the lead, so my parents brought her home to be with us in the manse where she lived ten years before she died.

Granny kept and passed on to my mother a letter a lady had written to grandpa, thanking him for his prayer for her healing. She'd made a remarkable recovery from a condition for which there'd been no medical remedy. He'd often prayed for the sick and it's good to have this one letter of praise to God. He was a man who truly loved people and he often read to us from St. John's epistles, the opening words of which I paraphrase at the end of *A Letter Comes to Light*.

From Nigeria to the Irish border

The poem *Time Voyage* is my childhood journey from shore to shore, and the move from childhood to adolescence. The two stanzas are symmetrical in form to highlight the parallels and contrasts between the two places and stages of my life.

Window is in memory of my dad, who met and married my mum soon after moving to Nigeria, arranging for his brother in South Africa to send a diamond ring in a mail package, which amazingly arrived with them unopened and in good time. Dad was the fixer of broken dolls in my early childhood, mender of cars and gadgets, and the designer and fitter of plastic sheet linings for windows in our draughty, cold manse, a decade before double glazing was in general use. He was the one who had taken us with him on journeys in canoes, paddling down the Niger, looking out for crocodiles, and we followed him up sandy beaches to the shade of a tree, watching out for snakes. There, a curious crowd would gather and listen, often for the first time, to the words of Jesus that dad and the Nigerian pastor would share.

During our time as a family in Nigeria, we all suffered bouts of malaria despite antimalarial medication, and before we were born, my mother had dengue fever. When at the age of eight, my sister suddenly took very ill with pneumonia at our home in the Igala region, we had an unexpected visit from a missionary doctor passing by with medical supplies, who produced the life-saving drug she needed. Another incident while playing in the garden was seeing a rabid dog, foaming at the mouth, advancing towards my little brother, who was rescued by the intervention of a quick-thinking Nigerian friend. In family prayer times, we gave thanks for God's presence and protection.

Mum was always dad's close partner in his ministry, both in Nigeria and in the two congregations just north of the border in Ireland, with families spread over a large area. She was the voluntary organist and secretary as well as leader of the women's group and an organization for girls. There were huge challenges for all those in pastoral ministry at that time. By the end of my dad's years there during the troubles, there was hardly a family who had not lost a loved one in a bomb or shooting, or suffered injury, or been forced out of their farms on the border by extremists.

After further ministry in County Tyrone, my parents retired to live in Bangor, and a few years later Dad was diagnosed with esophageal cancer. Throughout his illness he was gracious and uncomplaining, and till the end he was thinking of my mum's future needs as she cared for him. Even in his last days he was able to stay at home, thanks to the help of Marie Curie nurses, and I was there when he passed on. Certain people and events through our lives provide windows for us to see something more of God's grace, goodness and truth. Dad built my first window. I know he built many windows for a lot of other people in his life.

A new generation explores their heritage

Breath-taking is the arrival of my daughter's first child. Throughout the emotional upheaval of her pregnancy, she was determined to care for this new life with all her motherly instincts. With her, I'd prayed for the babe, remembering the words of Psalm 139: *For you created my inmost being; you knit me together in my mother's womb.*

The new baby in our home was calm and contented, and soon very alert and responsive. All the family helped to look after him while his mum completed her college qualifications. Like his mum, he was fun-loving and friendly, and from an early age showed exceptional artistic talent. Now, years later, he keeps alive his key interests in art and skateboarding and continues his studies in art at university.

For the Next Lap is for my second grandson. Even when he was little, he was a logical thinker and if given a task that he considered random, would want to know the reason. He has always liked order and routine, and enjoys the logic and ingenuity of mathematics, physics and computers, and the company of friends with similar interests. He is good at drawing and has a keen interest in fashion.

A highlight of our lives was when we went with Suzanne, her husband and family, to show Jay and Rhys their mother's Indonesian heritage, when they were eight and four years old. In Bali they swam in the pools and sea, took a boat to go snorkeling and look at the fish and the coral, explored mazes of craft shops and food stalls, visited bird and reptile parks, and saw traditional dances by moonlight to the gongs of the gamelan, while monkeys swung in trees nearby.

In Java we climbed up the spiral stone walls of the exquisitely carved ancient temple of Borobudur at dawn, visited a museum with Jurassic fossils, and went up the mountains to a volcano nature reserve and saw the flames from the smoking crater of Merapi. We sat at noodle bars in crowded cafes in the evenings under the gaze of other customers who often approached us to smile and talk.

We took the boys to see the garden in Salatiga, Central Java where their mother played when she was little and the house we'd lived in, now an office of the university. We used the local horse and cart transport as she had done to the school that she attended, and met people who knew her way back in time, like her dear friend Sunarsih, one of our past students, who had come all the way from Jakarta with her two children to meet with us.

In the cottage where we stayed, the boys watched with fascination the little creatures, ants on the floor marching to gather specks of sugar, cockroaches scuttling in the bathroom and lizards that raced with ease up walls, then waited motionless to prey on any unsuspecting insect that approached. At night we all took refuge from mosquitoes under the nets we strung over our beds.

After two weeks, the rest of the family flew home and Jim and I stayed on to lead English language teacher training courses in Salatiga and then in Timor. There we stayed with our good friend Elsye, a Timorese minister, and her Irish husband Barry McCroskery. They'd met while studying theology in Belfast and now worked together in the church and university in Kupang, Timor.

One of the Indonesian church's strengths is to value and benefit from having many women as ministers of congregations. We went with Elsye and Barry to visit students on placements in remote, rural areas. Seeing the simplicity of the living conditions and the commitment in pastoral ministry of church ministers was a deeply moving experience.

Several years after that Indonesian trip, our granddaughter Ruby was born. The final poem here, *Very Special Gemstone*, is for her. As every child should be, she is treasured as a unique and beautiful gem, and is very sociable and artistic like Suzanne, her mum, who with her warmth and kindness reaches out to everyone she meets.

6

Still Small Voice

I've carefully read the story of Elijah so often,
and so often has it given me strength.

—VINCENT VAN GOGH, LETTER TO THEO, 31 MAY 1877

ROYAL BIRTH

When he arrived
no palace announcement,
press release or photo shoot,
no band, town crier,
bell ringer or gun salute.
When the angels sang, earth was asleep,

took no notice
of the music or dancing in the night sky,
the pyrotechnic extravaganza
of light and sound.
Insomniacs closed their eyes,
thinking they were dreaming.

Only lambs responded, bleating,
and shepherds jumped up and listened
to long-awaited news—
promise of generations,
centuries, millennia—
joy and peace to the world.

When Jupiter and Saturn
joined in the constellation of Pisces
and beamed over Jerusalem
no one blinked an eye.
Only a few foreign dignitaries
set out on camels in search for a King.

Provincial royalty
took their inquiry seriously,
consulted maps and archivists,
gave them a sign, an order:
go and come back as informers.

But agents are God's speciality:

when the wise sons of Sheba
found with joy the son of David,
truth illumined in a star,
the assassin's plot
was floodlit in a dream,
and they left by a secret route.

So the humble family,
firstborn wrapped,
and with gold and spices,
hidden in a cloak,
fled through the shadows
from the first of their oppressors.

Death decree. Infanticide.
Targets in their own country.
Escapees, refugees.
Migrants, on a long journey
far from home, the green fields
and fruit trees, to cross the border.

When they arrived,
no welcome.
Just a tent
in a desert.

STILL SMALL VOICE

Threatened, hunted, terrified,
forsaken and betrayed,
he fled across the desert land,
then fell exhausted on the sand
and in a thorn-tree's meagre shade
cried out, *My life is over.*

Get up and eat,
a voice replied,
a hand upon his shoulder.
Fresh bread lay warm
upon a stone
beside a jar of water.

With hunger eased
his hope increased,
for forty days he clambered
and trudged the heights,
then in a cave
endured a storm that battered

and tumbled rocks,
crumbled cliffs
and heavy boulders shattered;
fierce flames leapt up
the mountain shook
and all of nature trembled.

Then silence.

And in the darkness
just a breath,
the softest whisper came
through dust and ash,

so faintly heard
the calling of a name,

Why are you here, Elijah?
My child, what do you fear?
You're not alone, Elijah,
servant of God, most dear.
Go in the name of Jehovah,
the holy one is near.

Stronger than any wind or storm
or force that shakes the world,
Breath of life
within the cave
within my heart
his word.

HOUSE OF PEACE

Let there be
no weapons of war
in my home

Let there be
no instruments
that wound

no words that cut like blades
no pointed, sharp complaint
no stab of blame
no stone of judgment aimed
no bullet of resentment.

Each weapon handed in to Christ
who suffered to bring peace

He lets us have new hearts of love
with healing words and deeds.

LIKE THE SUN

Climb the mountain, seek the one
whose glory is the rising sun

Cocoon of cloud as earth meets heaven,
from deep within a voice calls out:

My Son, beloved one, is here
He is my joy—
Take heed, listen!

He who conquers death
shall set you free on wings of faith.

Friend to Moses face to face
the whisper in Elijah's ear
the touch that banished fear with grace

We are transformed
as you draw near.

THIS IS THE HOUR

This is the hour for your will to be done Lord,
the one-of a-kind hour of life,
each person I meet, each incident
opening a door to bring Christ in.

This is the vital hour of kingdom-come,
the hour for the shining of hope,
the hour to believe and begin renewal,
to open a window to love eternal.

This is the transformative hour of forgiveness,
of thankfulness for grace;
this is the hour you have given us
to be a bridge, a gateway to peace.

I HEARD A STORY

I heard a story once
when I was very small
how the finger of the Lord
had written on a wall
and on a mountain top
he took a slab of stone
and wrote a guide to life,
love's code for everyone.

So many people now
stand accused in shame
but the finger of the Lord
writes in the dust again,
Let he who has no sin
cast the first stone of blame.
The word of Christ forgives;
we trust in him and live.

The faithful prophets spoke
in poems long ago
inscribed on precious scrolls
so all can hear and know
how the hand of God is strong
for he planned it all along
to heal and save a broken world
through the offering of his Son.

Write with your Spirit on my heart,
touch the dust and stone,
let all the pages of my life
make your glory known.

OIL OF MYRRH REFLECTIONS

1. Wounded Healer

From wounded trees,
bark penetrated
to reach the living sapwood.

The trees weep
precious healing oil,
fragrance, incense,

a costly harvest.
With no sap,
heartwood left untouched.

2. Oil of Holiness (Exod 30:22–31)

The spices, cinnamon bark and flower,
ground with a root, and the sap of myrrh
and the oil of olive, pure and fragrant,
to a blend, unique and sacred,

the oil of the Lord and his anointed,
priests, prophets, kings that he appointed.
The tent with oil, consecrated,
lamp and furniture dedicated

so all the people
who gathered would share
the beauty of holiness,
God's presence there.

3. Living in Unity (Ps 133: like precious oil poured out)

As the sacred oil
from precious perfumes
poured on Aaron's head,
flowing down his robes—
Let us live in unity
to enjoy your blessing, O Lord.

As the melting snow descended
from Hermon's slopes
filling the river Jordan,
replenishing the valleys—
Let us move as one,
bringing fruitfulness, O Lord.

As the dew falling
on Sinai's desert
brought manna to Israel's children—
Come to us,
gather us together, O Lord.

As the oils were blended
to a unique fragrance—
Unite us
to be poured out in love,
the aroma of Christ's life
for the world.

.

For you, Lord, are the single source
of our humanity,
of creativity,
the one Divinity,

so let us flow as one river

of living water
through this dry land,
use our gifts together,
share bread with our neighbor,
as you have planned.

Father, fountain and source of all fruitfulness,
Son, bread of life, offering forgiveness,
Spirit, oil of comfort and gladness—
Three together, the one true God,

we trust and delight in you,
dwell and unite in you,
Trinity, Unity,
Fellowship of love.

4. Bridal Preparation

Through the palace gates,
monumental mansion
of Xerxes the Great—
tall and bearded with his parasol and fan,
Persian Emperor of lands
from India to Ethiopia—
Hebrew girl, Hadassah, Myrtle,
daughter of captive nation,
was taken,

flower blown in by the wind
among imposing colonnades and terraces
paved with marble,
mother-of-pearl and turquoise,
rows of silver couches,
goblets, banquets,

to the inner harem,
fine-spun garments,
bowls of dates and honey.

Her name in Persia, Esther, Star,
open sky above her,
slave Hegai to stand on guard,
towering walls surround her.

Bridal Queen to be prepared
with finest beauty treatment,
her body toned with oil of myrrh
and balsam, precious ointment.

Choice of an imperial king
to be his pride and bliss,

chosen by the King of Kings
for such a time as this.

Come to us our bridegroom King
with robes of loving-kindness,
prepare us for your wedding feast,
your presence is our fragrance,
your peace, the pearls you give to share,
to treasure, not destroy,
your ring, the seal of faithfulness,
your love, our crowning joy.

To this our world,
the King of Love has sent the invitation
to set us free to be his bride,
we come from every nation.

5. Myrrh, Fragrance of Lovers (An arrangement of images from *Song of Songs*)

Like the pleasure of wine,
like perfume poured out
so precious your name.[1]

My lover is to me
a sachet of myrrh
resting between my breasts.[2]

His gentle lips
are like lilies
dripping with myrrh.[3]

I arose for my lover
and my hands dripped with myrrh
as I opened the lock.[4]

To the garden of spice
come my beloved,
taste its choice fruits.[5]

You who dwell in the gardens,
let me hear your voice.
Come away like a gazelle
on the spice-laden mountains.[6]

Blow, spring breeze,
let the fragrance flow

1. Song 1:2–3
2. Song 1:13
3. Song 5:13
4. Song 5:5
5. Song 4:16
6. Song 8:13–14

from the incense trees,
the myrrh and aloe.[7]

Let love seal our hearts forever,
blazing fire unquenched by water.
Rushing rivers cannot wash
love's flame away.[8]

7. Song 4:13–16
8. Song 8:6–7

6. Mary's Treasure (Luke 2:41–52; Prov 2:4; 8:10–11)

First moment of panic
as if pierced by a blade.
Assumed he was with the rest of the family,
safe in a crowd of friends as we left to go home.
Suddenly aware of his absence.
Worst fear of a parent.
Missing child.

Retrace our steps.
Asking folk all along the way.
Anxiety mounting. Sleepless night
under the stars, second day.
Guilt. Frustration. Trying to remember.
Last seen. Clothes worn.
Final words spoken.

Flashback to the day of birth.
Visitors on a journey, searching, finding.
Strangeness of gift, resinous fragrance
overpowering the stench of cattle.
Swaddled baby, or a body wrapped in linen
with oil of myrrh for burial?
Where would this Passover journey lead?

What value has gold compared with life?
Our child, David and Bathsheba's golden line.
Words of their son, Solomon:
Seek wisdom like hidden treasure;
choose knowledge rather than gold.
Like seeking our child—heart, soul and mind.
Three-day-search like years.

Frankincense—aroma of prayer—

prophetic gift? Press on to find.
Hearts racing at the temple gates.
Entering the courts. Scanning the faces.
Men of learning. See! There in the midst—
animated face of a boy—*Son, you're alive!*
We thought we'd lost you!

Tears of relief and joy. Warm embraces.
Plying him with questions.
Answer of the Son, surprised we didn't know
he must be in his Father's house,
searching for wisdom, exploring his identity,
the big plan of things,
at only twelve years old.

First step away from us and our protection.
Big step forward for us on a faith journey.
Child we love, refusing to be a crowd follower,
choosing the unsafe route,
unafraid of authority.
Letting our son grow trusting in God's provision,
follow his lead.

I ponder and store these treasures in my heart.
Wisdom found in times of greatest need
is like rubies
mined from deep in the earth's crust,
a precious pearl
lifted by a diver
from the darkness of the ocean bed.

SHARING MARY'S PRAYER

I searched for you I thought I'd lost
I found you in the house of prayer
Your words I treasure in my heart
And when I'm lost I'll find you there.

REFLECTION

Creative communication and God's unfolding drama

Through the years, as I've thought about life as being part of God's great unfolding drama, I've wanted to express this story in a variety of ways. With groups of all ages, the enthusiasm of young children and the imagination of the old, we've read, mimed, acted and danced in schools and halls and churches here in Ireland and overseas. I've taught children Bible stories through drama in Javanese villages amid rice terraces, and adults in a church courtyard in a Japanese town. I've led workshops at an international ladies' retreat at a quiet lake in Java, and with students learning to teach the Bible to children in crowded classrooms. With a team from Ireland we've been to churches on beaches and hillsides of other Indonesian islands, crossing language barriers with songs and stories in mime.

Finding imaginative ways to communicate Christian truths and values was also the goal of the books of Sunday School materials a team of us prepared for use in Indonesia. A story about Jesus remains just a story until we show how the person of Christ relates to our lives, and how we fit into the big picture of God's plan. For any age group, the dramatized reading of short scenes or poems can help with understanding the layers of meaning in a Bible passage and its message for us today, and can be part of liturgy, an expression of prayer or worship.

The planning and writing of any script or poem linked with the Bible has always evolved from careful reading and study of the passages, and listening to how God is speaking. It's also good to rediscover the Jewish roots of worship with movement in praise, and the presence of visual and tactile objects as symbols. I noticed in Java how student teachers in my classes took part in drama workshops with enthusiasm. Although for many of them it was their first experience of that kind of activity in a Christian Education setting, they were well used to dance drama and puppet theater that are part of Javanese and Balinese culture.

The God who speaks

The title of the poem, *Still Small Voice*, a familiar phrase from the King James Bible, in some modern translations of the Bible is "a gentle whisper," or in the New Revised Standard, "a sound of sheer silence." It describes the way God spoke to Elijah when he was running from Ahab and Jezebel who sought his life (1 Kings 19:11–13). God cared for Elijah even in the darkness of exhaustion and depression. He is often present where we least expect to find him, speaking in a voice so ordinary, we are slow to recognize it as his. Sometimes we need to look for a quiet place so we can learn to hear his voice, his wisdom and guidance, his quiet word of reassurance within us. As I read the Elijah story at a church retreat, I thought of how it speaks of God's intimate compassion, choosing to reveal his holy presence, his glory, in such a humble, gentle way. As a response, I wrote the poem *Still Small Voice*. It could be read in chorus, perhaps by children, with direct speech parts spoken by individual voices. For dramatic purposes, sound effects might be added.

In a similar way, the account in the Bible of God's compassion for the grief-stricken migrants, Naomi and Ruth, is encouraging and inspiring, and I have used *The Dramatised Bible*, (ed. Michael Perry, Marshall Pickering, 1989) to present the Book of Ruth over four weeks of congregational worship services. *The Dramatised Bible*, with short passages each written for various voice parts, is a very useful resource for readings.

I Heard a Story is a reflection on ways God has spoken in the past, and how he still speaks. It links with various Scriptures (Dan 5:1–5; Exod 31:18; John 8:1–11). Also in my thoughts were the verses: *In the past God spoke to our forefathers through the prophets . . . but in these last days he has spoken to us by his Son* (Heb 1:1) and, *You show that you are a letter from Christ, the result of our ministry, written not with ink but with the Spirit of the living God, not on tablets of stone but on tablets of human hearts* (2 Cor 3:3). This was fulfilling an Old Testament promise (Jer 31:33). The New Testament constantly refers to the Old to show that the coming of Christ fulfils the great promises made in the Old Covenant.

Like the Sun arose from reading the passage about the transfiguration, which links Moses and Elijah, the law and the prophets of the Old Testament, with Jesus and the apostles (Matt 17:1–8; Mark 9:2–8; Luke 9:28–36). The Greek word used in Matthew and Mark, *metamorphoo*, is also found in Romans 12:2 and in 2 Corinthians 3:18, referring to believers being transformed by Christ (as opposed to being conformed to the world). St. Luke records that Jesus spoke with Moses and Elijah about his death and resurrection. I thought of the cloud mentioned in these texts as like a cocoon that surrounds us as we, often fearful like the disciples, struggle for understanding, and the idea of wings that break through being a moment of truth and transition into light and freedom.

The message of the New Testament is that we are all called to fulfill the potential we have as human beings with various gifts and personalities, and that the life Christ gives can transform our natural life because he shares with us the uncreated life of his Holy Spirit.

The big picture

In our contemporary world, few people seem to have knowledge of the Bible, although it is accessible to us as never before through free apps on our phones. Some don't give it a second thought because they think it is much too difficult to understand, while others diminish its scope by describing it as just a collection of stories. Although the stories are wonderfully told and worth reading for their own sake, like the poetry or prophecy, they are all part of one central message that runs through the Bible, like a river with many tributaries.

The key is to keep sight of the Big Story, that the God of love establishes his kingdom on earth by restoring people to be one family, just as a loving parent looks for a lost child, or as a lover seeks his beloved. God's drama unfolds in the Old Testament through choosing a people to trust him and show his goodness to the world, a purpose only fulfilled in the coming of Christ as Savior for all nations, to be completed when he returns to restore all things in the new heaven and the new earth. As C.S. Lewis explains in his book, *Miracles*, God's incarnation as the historical Jesus, who died and was raised, is "the grand miracle" on which the whole of God's story turns.

The core of Jesus's teaching in John's Gospel is that the Son of God came to show us the Father's love, and to invite human beings to enter into the community of love that he experiences in the Trinity, with the Father and the Holy Spirit. He wants our relationships to reflect the love of that divine community. It is this I have in mind in the poem-prayer, *Living in Unity*. My starting point is from Psalm 133:1: *How good and pleasant it is when brothers live together in unity! It is like precious oil poured on the head.*

In our post-Christian culture, it is the loss of being part of a big picture that has led to the frequent view that life is meaningless. When there is little sense of belonging or significance, feelings of emptiness and low self-worth cause many to stifle emotional pain in harmful ways.

Symbols linking old and new

The recurring images in the Bible have long fascinated me. *Oil of Myrrh Reflections* grew from thinking about how fragrance is used as an image of the followers of Christ (2 Cor 2:14—16). In their introduction to the *Dictionary of Biblical Imagery* (IVP, 1998), the editors write: "a systematic treatment of the images and motifs in the Bible allows us to see the unity and progression of the Bible. Unity emerges when we see that many of the master images pervade it from beginning to end." Oil is mentioned around two hundred times in the Bible, as this Dictionary points out, often referring to the common olive oil used daily for making bread, anointing dry or wounded skin, or as the common fuel for lamps. It also had special uses, blended with rare perfumes like myrrh for body lotions or anointing oil, or for ceremonial use in the temple (as in my poem *Oil of Holiness*). Tracing the uses of the image allows us to see how the New Testament builds on and fulfills what has been foreshadowed in the Old Testament. Jesus was known as "the anointed one", not with oil but with God's Spirit and power (Acts 10:38), and his followers are described as receiving, through him, the Holy Spirit's anointing (2 Cor 1:21–22).

Bridal Preparation is based on the account from the book of Esther (chapters 1–2) of how Mordecai brought Esther, his adopted daughter, to the palace when the king announced that he wanted a new queen. The king chose Esther above the other maidens, and later in her position as queen she was able to intervene on behalf of the Jewish people when a plot was devised to kill them. It was Mordecai who persuaded Esther with the words: *and who knows but that you have come to your royal position for such a time as this?* (Esth 4:14).

Psalm 45 is a song for a bridegroom king, most likely King David, but also applied to the Messiah, Son of David: *God, your God, has anointed you with the oil of gladness . . . your robes are all fragrant with myrrh and aloes and cassia.* Paul uses the metaphor of Christ as bridegroom and God's people as his bride, and the symbolism culminates in the wedding supper of the Lamb described in the book of Revelation (19:6–9).

Fragrance of Lovers is an arrangement of images linked with the perfume myrrh in *Song of Songs*. This biblical book of poetry celebrates ideal love and commitment between a lover and his bride. It has long been seen as having a spiritual parallel in the love between God and his people.

Peacemakers

House of Peace originated from reading a Celtic poem about peace, at a time of conflict within my own family. When I wrote it, I pinned it on my bathroom wall.

This is the Hour is my meditation after reading an excerpt from *The Diary of a Russian Priest* by Alexander Elchaninov (Faber, 1967), who highlights the importance of seeing the present hour as the one in which we do God's will.

In *Royal Birth*, I reflect on the birth of the Christ child and his family fleeing King Herod's decree, taking refuge in Egypt. I think of the many displaced families who've come to our country and are not always accepted by the community they live among. Jesus has suffered as they have. I know that they too, made in God's image, are loved and precious in his sight. Because Christ first loved us and calls us his friends, we are to show love for God by loving others. If we are to follow the Jesus of the Gospels, this must surely include showing friendship to those whose backgrounds are very different from our own, even to those who are perceived by some as enemies. Because Jesus came to make peace for us, we are called to be peacemakers, and to share the good news of shalom. The Hebrew word 'shalom' implies complete well-being of body, mind and spirit. This comes through restored relationships with God, ourselves, and others.

7

Icelandic Cloud

Find things beautiful as much as you can,
most people find too little beautiful.

—Vincent Van Gogh, letter to Theo, January 1874

ICELANDIC CLOUD

So alive
eagle in full flight
you filled our sky
to you our world belonged.
So free, so strong
you lived to move
and breathe
and now
all motion
all
is gone.

Across the sea a mountain flings
its ice and fire:
the skies—all flights—are closed.

Across the land the ballots all are taken.
What's firm one day
the very next is shaken.

In the white ward, moving
to make room for another,
they clear the belongings
(empty trainers and a few limp clothes)
into a plastic bag
and place it
in the arms of his wife, his lover—

she barely knows
he's gone—and she, the young widow
is handed a manual,
Information for the Family of the Deceased.

It's dawn. We leave.
Three days and four nights
of hope and disbelief
behind us.

Before us
ceaseless days and nights.
Ice-shock.
Fire of grief.

COLLAGE

Arranged across the mountains
like hearts, like tears
petals

dropped from a bride's bouquet
that day
(I wanted them to last)

kept in a box to dry
forgotten
found after years

unpacked, pressed and fixed
as leaves of gold
a sunset sky—

landscape
in the shadow
a wedding portrait cast.

I return
unseal the box, find
and touch again the freesia

once fresh
artistically entwined
admired and kissed

turn and lift
the last few parchment pieces
shed and shift

and shape these words
to make
this—

one more collage—
cut and pasted foliage
across a distant range

from delicate
handpicked
hand-held
discarded flowers.

NINETY CANDLES

I used to fear what life would be
were I to lose you
as if some gust of wind would carry you away
like a balloon with the string snapped from my hand,
or a castle tumbled by some careless finger,
the fortress scattered, block by wooden block,
or a brightly painted rainbow ruined
by murky water spilt from a toppled jar.

On arid terracotta soil
with spiky, towering termite mounds,
you read to us and showed us other worlds,
the story of Green Gables, Anne, adopted child
whose loss of Matthew (like your father, left behind)
gave us our first glimpse of death.
We watched your tears flow on the pages,
flooding our hearts in a river of sadness.

You carried us, nurtured us,
fed us, led us,
put us first above all your needs.
What would our days have been without your strength and comfort
or slipping into sleep without your song?

The lights are flashing on the Christmas tree
like twinkling memories of names and faces.
We'll light the ninety candles on your cake.
They'll sparkle, melt and trickle like the snow
that falls in flakes on windows in the starlight.
Through the glass we glimpse the Milky Way
and see our years on earth are just a ray
that shimmers for a moment and is gone;

the wonder is its source and destiny—
I'll find them in the Shining of the One

Who carries us, nurtures us,
feeds us, leads us,
cares for us his children in all our human need.
How could we live a day without such lovingkindness
or sleep and rise again without a song?

LAST TIME

The last time I was here I was with Harry.
We drive and stop and every place
becomes a meeting point with him.
The many times she's seen this road
all those twenty years since he departed
are irrelevant, discarded landscapes
like the pictures (now boxed up)
we took down from the walls of her beloved home,
emptied, a whole year ago
that day she moved.

Today, another day, I sit with her
in the carefully ordered, compact room
she has to call her home.
I look beyond the reclining chair, favorite rug,
cut glass vase, familiar coffee mug,
selected stack of books, photos of family, Rusty dog
so static in his frame,
beyond the lines of her declining years,
the fragile body, frame so bent and worn,
beyond this sketch, this jot

of who you are—
to see the whole,
the bright impasto portrait of your soul,
your mind so agile all those years,
the rooms you filled
with home-baked pies and puddings,
hand-knit winter woollies, sewing, storytelling, song,
your laughter, your piano,
the lives your wise and faith-filled words
made strong

and know that I am here
to climb with you
the rugged, foot-worn track ahead
that soon you'll leave
behind.

THE BAY

In that fleeting
not unexpected
yet shocking moment
the last time
I saw your face

I felt the world sway
as I froze in the doorway
of your silent, sea-view room
my heart rapidly beating
while yours that so loved stood still.

Still now at the edge of the open bay
as the sea heaves
and the sky is wreathed in purple and grey
and the cries of the redshank
rise in the onshore breeze

that last moment lost
fled as a breath
returns unexpectedly
sharp as the chill in the salty air
dull as the tug of a silent tear.

LIFE POEM

You spoke so feebly
a poem of such strength
those last two days in January:

Beautiful (the sun shines on the sea)
Lovely (a dog walks past your window)
Don't kill yourself (to the nurse who lifts and tucks you in)
So kind (I hold a straw to your dry lips and you sip water)

Language of praise never lost,
rooted in heaven.

HIGHS AND LOWS

My husband and I, separated,
I mean I've lost him.
Both of us alone.
I was taking photos—
he walked on—
path divided—out of sight—
hasn't got his phone—

sentences in scissor snips
to the guide at the fort
with the splendid view
of the Spanish port
I would have swapped right then for home.

Pinpoint of fear, the threat of a hypo
only the afflicted understand,
induced tides of insulin,
the glucose dive and flow.

Unfazed, smooth as glass reply,
No café on that path, sorry.
It's a long loop back to this gate.
Is there a meeting point you've planned?
Go there and wait.
Good luck!

I prayed
words that flew like bubbles
and blew across the valley,
ribbons, reels of petitions,
loops spoken back to me:
Unravel the knots.
Make the pattern plain.

Unwind the thread of the plot.
Air ambulance. Stretcher. Helicopter.
Scenarios swirl in the brain.

And when I circled again
to the tip of the mountain cable
that rose like a needle,
the point where we started
and all seemed stable—
he was there. Unperturbed.
How is it possible? Where? Why?

And as we departed, reunited—
dropping over thimble trees,
the sugar dust of flowers,
swinging over threading paths,
spools and cubes
and chocolate blocks of towers—
encased in the glass bubble of the cable car,

I knew that joy had overflowed and filled
the whole wide sphere of the encompassing sky.

REFLECTION

Sudden Loss

In the face of life-threatening situations, Paul writes: *the one who raised the Lord Jesus from the dead will also raise us with Jesus . . . Therefore we do not lose heart. Though outwardly we are wasting away, yet inwardly we are being renewed day by day. For our light and momentary troubles are achieving for us an eternal glory that far outweighs them all. So we fix our eyes not on what is seen, but on what is unseen. For what is seen is temporary, but what is unseen is eternal* (2 Cor 4:14–16).

Paul knew better than most that in human life there is nothing *light and momentary* about suffering. It can be overwhelming in its pain. Yet he tries to find a scale by which we can measure it, and the only scale that matters is the weight of eternal glory that Jesus has entered into and to which he will bring his followers through his resurrection.

With the eruption in 2010 of the Icelandic volcano, Eyjafjallajökull, the flight Jim's brother Mike was due to take from Belfast to London was cancelled, so he was at home after his routine jog. He'd phoned us the night before to ask about Jim who'd just had health check. Keen on sport, Mike had met his wife Ann, a Londoner, through hockey, and coached his girls in table tennis in which he'd represented Ireland.

It was a huge shock then, that Mike, despite his fitness, collapsed that morning at home and was unconscious in hospital having suffered cardiac arrest from which he never recovered. I wrote the poem *Icelandic Cloud* just after this. Two of Mike and Ann's daughters, Susie and Natasha, were about to do important school exams, and Jemma, the eldest, was just a year into university in England. It was a time of enormous loss and grief for them. They could only aim to do what they knew their father would want, live life to the full as they always had done. He had followed the Christian path that he'd begun early in life, and he and his family were part of the life of the local church. Ann's Jewish parents escaped the holocaust as teenagers by fleeing from Nazi Germany to England.

She's an exceptionally capable and caring person and she and Mike were united in all they did, especially in their commitment to the girls. Mike was a central part of their lives, and yet Ann's strength and close ties with her daughters have enabled her to be the mainstay of the family ever since.

Mike's death was a great loss to his mum Barbara, a wonderfully gracious lady whose love and goodness shone through in all she did, and who lived courageously with Parkinson's disease in her later years, and to his sister Janet and her family, Paul, Andy and Chrissie. Although Mike commuted to work in London each week, when he was back home in Bangor on Saturdays, he never missed a get-together for coffee with all of us. He always asked about everyone and shared his insights and great sense of humor. At the height of his career working in Reuters, he was unassuming and approachable, able to relate to anyone.

Not long after his death, I dreamt Mike broke out of his coffin, dug his way out of the earth's soil and stood up alive and well. Just like Mike, I thought in the dream, as if death could hold him down. When I awoke and remembered the reality, the shock and sadness came back. But then I knew that the dream was also true: he was alive and present with the Lord in whom he trusted, just as Jesus told Martha and Mary before raising their brother from the dead, *I am the resurrection and the life. He who believes in me will live, even though he dies* (John 11:25).

Making new pictures

The poem *Collage* reflects on relationships that fall apart, and attempts to find meaning in brokenness.

Separation in all its forms, the loss and sorrow it brings, is part of human existence, but when it comes close to us and affects the people we love, we enter into a whole new realm of pain. We are then able to understand, in a way we couldn't have done before, people who go through the same heartache. The God of compassion suffers with us and in times of sorrow and disappointment helps bring something positive out of painful experiences.

The pieces of life can come together to make new pictures, with healing and renewed hope.

Slipping away

The slow separation that results when a parent slips into the twilight, and dementia begins to set in, is a painful experience in a family, as alluded to in *Ninety Candles* and *Last Time*. At the stage when mum was getting confused, it helped to recognize her as she always had been, a person with an interest in people and a great sense of humor. All her life my mum had loved books, and letters she'd been reading about Christians in difficult situations across the world, many of whom she helped to support financially, would be spread out on her table for prayer.

She moved to residential care just as the gathering fog in her mind was preventing her from living unaided. Yet she was still reading. She would've laughed if she'd realized she was reading the same page over and over, and telling me with delight every day: "Look! This book is all about the saints in Ireland." I liked the thought of her getting to meet those Celtic saints and also the ones she'd known in her years in Nigeria, and the people of faith from other places whose lives she'd followed in all her letters. I knew she'd join with enthusiasm the praises of every tribe and nation gathered together in that life to come

Her condition declined quite rapidly after that, though at the time it seemed to me like a slow death, a loss, piece by piece, of the personal independence she'd valued so highly, never wanting to cause trouble for anyone. Yet we were blessed that at the end she still recognized us even though she muddled our names. All memories of the past she used to share with me had died away, and this I missed, but even in the last few days she was faintly aware of her surroundings and able to communicate slightly. *Life Poem* shows how her last few words sum up the life attitude of Molly Clarke, my mother. It was heart failure and a fall that caused the final slipping away. Friends who knew her when they were young told me she'd been their spiritual mother. I knew they shared in our family's sorrow, just as we'd all been so greatly blessed by her.

Trust

Highs and Lows relates one of many experiences Jim and I have had with type one diabetes, and the anxiety that can arise for me as a partner if I think sudden low blood sugar may occur. It's a reminder to me to trust in God every day rather than letting fear take hold.

We've been very aware of God's protection in many instances. One that stands out is the day our first grandchild was born. I waited in the hospital in the evening with Suzanne and the baby, as my husband faced the storm outside to drive home in the car. I remember feeling tense after he left, hoping he'd get supper on time, but I knew I could pray for him, and so I did. Later his brother Mike phoned our house from London to see how things were, and hearing Jim's slurred speech, he phoned their sister Janet, who immediately drove to the house and found Jim unconscious from a hypo. She was able to revive him in time. The night our first grandchild was born could also have been the night the baby lost his granddad.

I'm so thankful when I think of the countless ways Jim has been a rock to our grandchildren, just as he is to his children and to me, supporting us with his wisdom, faith and practical deeds of kindness and generosity. He's been their guide in all things educational, an ever-patient listener and mentor through challenging times, always willing to give of his time and energy where needed. Although he is extremely organized and efficient, the delicate balance involved in having diabetes requires constant vigilance. This has made us appreciate that life is a daily gift, and that we live each day depending on God, determined to *fix our eyes on Jesus, the author and perfecter of our faith* (Heb 12:2). In other words Paul says, *we live by faith, not by sight* (2 Cor 5:7).

In times of sorrow and loss I've found encouragement in these words which refer to the hope we have in the resurrection: *Dear friends, now we are children of God, and what we will be has not yet been made known. But we know that when he appears, we shall be like him, for we shall see him as he is* (1 John 3:2).

8

In the Picture

There is something of Rembrandt in the Gospel,
or something of the Gospel in Rembrandt, as you like it—
it comes to the same, provided that one understands it rightly.
—Vincent Van Gogh, letter to Theo, 22 June 1880)

WOMAN IN THE PICTURE (Bathsheba with King David's Letter, Rembrandt, 1654)

Picture a gown laid out and waiting,
its folds, a sea of amber,
a bowl in the kneeling servant's hands,
in the shadows, her face tender,
she washes a woman's feet with fragrant water.
The woman watches, wants this frame to linger,

she knows her feet must travel on
to the jeweled chamber;
the letter with his seal is fixed,
she holds it in her finger.
Will water wash away the stain
or herbal essence heal the guilt and pain?

In his mind she is milk and honey.
He thirsts for her as for sparkling wine.
Sunlight caught her as she bathed,
brushed her with gold, the curve of her body,
a touch of rose on her breast,
like the dawn as he gazed from his open window.

No glimmer of sunrise in the night of heartache.
No moon to shine on her marriage bed.
A past life lost,
a union ground to dust.
Lust. Shock.
Only the sound of trickling water.

She knows the season of the sweet fig,
the laden vine,
the juice that flows from the pomegranate
and the crushed olive,

but if she bears fruit,
what life will she sustain?

Whose love casts no blame?
Whose family line?
Generations wait in wonder
for the Morning Star to shine.

HENDRICKJE IN THE PICTURE

Christ's servant would have washed your feet
Hendrickje
artist's Bathsheba
unwed
bearing unborn child

instead
you hold the elders' letter
called to stand beneath their gaze
called whore
cast out

yet in the artist's light
restored
with lasting grace.

CHILD IN THE PICTURE (Simeon with the Christ Child in the Temple, Rembrandt, 1669)

Titia,
your father Titus never lived to know or hold you
yet here you are, cradled in the ancient prophet's arms.

He, who knew so well
Abraham and Isaac, Jacob,
Joseph, Moses, Samson, David,
and with his brush and palette
brought them back to life,
now, though nearly blind,
beholds the glory, revelation,
promised child,
hope of humankind.

Titia,
your grandfather
lost his wife and all their children.
Down through the years he searched for light
in the darkness.
Now in his last days he sees God's gift,
his splendid image, radiant in you,
light of his world.

Titia,
priceless new-born daughter,
what sword has pierced the soul of Magdalena,
your own mother?
Her days too are numbered.
She cries, "What will become of you?"
Yet you are blessed.

He makes his face to shine upon you.
With gifted hand he separates light
from the darkness.
He has clothed you with light,
child of an eternal kingdom,
desire of his own heart
before he departs
this world, blessing you,
in peace.

As Simeon in the arms of death
holds the babe, breath of life,
gazing also face to face,
artist and the child of grace;
streams of glory, light of heaven
touches earth.

REFLECTION

Rembrandt's late art

A visit to any large town or city for me means searching out its art galleries. Several years ago, the National Gallery in London held an exhibition entitled *Rembrandt: The Late Works, 1650–1669*. The reviewer in *The Guardian* newspaper (19 October 2014) tried hard to find words to describe the magnificence of Rembrandt's late art: "dark, impassioned, magnificently defiant, at the pitch of his originality — and bewilderingly unexpected in the spectacle of his irrepressible power and variety." My poems, *Woman in the Picture, Hendrickje in the Picture* and *Child in the Picture* are my responses to two of Rembrandt's late works.

Bathsheba with King David's Letter

Rembrandt's painting, *Bathsheba with King David's Letter* (1654, Louvre, Paris), has as its subject the woman whose story is told in The Second Book of Samuel (11:2–4). King David saw a woman bathing as he walked in the early morning on his palace roof. He found out that she was Bathsheba, wife of Uriah, a soldier who was away fighting in the king's army. David sent his messengers to fetch her. Rembrandt's painting focuses only on Bathsheba, her life-size body and facial expression, seated holding a letter, evidently from the king summoning her to sleep with him. Rembrandt shows sensitivity to Bathsheba's conflicting emotions as she ponders the outcome of submitting to the king, and I reflect on this in *Woman in the Picture*.

By painting Bathsheba realistically in the nude, Rembrandt broke away from the classical idealized portrayal of the female figure. He places the viewer in the position of voyeur, as King David had been, at the same time drawing attention to her emotional quandary. In Rembrandt's portraits he always has the wonderful gift of drawing his viewer into the picture. The story continues that Bathsheba became pregnant with King David's child. After sending Uriah into the frontline of battle to have him killed, David married

Bathsheba. Later the prophet Nathan brought God's word of rebuke and judgment to David. St. Matthew's radical genealogy of Jesus insists on reminding us that Bathsheba was Uriah's wife, as well as the mother of King Solomon and the ancestor of Jesus himself.

Hendrickje in the Picture addresses Hendrickje Stoffels, Rembrandt's housekeeper and later his common-law wife. She is considered to be the sitter for Rembrandt's *Bathsheba* as well as for *A Woman Bathing in a Stream*, painted the same year. In 1654 when Rembrandt was working on these paintings, Hendrickje was pregnant with his child. Because of this, she was called by the Reformed Church Council to answer to the charge that she had "committed the acts of a whore with Rembrandt the painter," and her right to communion was taken from her. The artist himself was not a member of that church, so outside their jurisdiction, although it was no doubt more common to condemn the woman than the man. The link between Hendrickje's situation and Bathsheba's letter in the picture is clear.

Perhaps Rembrandt saw his own connection with David and Bathsheba, in that he the powerful male was taking advantage of Hendrickje, his housekeeper, who was hardly in a position financially to refuse him. However, I wonder if this painting was also an expression of Rembrandt's defiance at the church's lack of sympathy for Hendrickje. Perhaps the servant washing Bathsheba's feet was a hint at the example of servant leadership that Jesus gave his disciples, in contrast to a judgmental attitude. Possibly the painting was also the artist's invitation to his partner to accept and celebrate her sensuality and fertility without shame. Rembrandt was certainly a very independent and defiant personality.

Simeon with the Christ Child in the Temple

The Rembrandt of the later works was suffering tragedy after tragedy. His wife Saskia had died in 1642 at the age of 30, and of their four children, only their son Titus survived. Hendrickje died in 1663. Rembrandt himself had just become bankrupt and was fighting battles in the law courts.

While he was painting *Simeon with the Christ Child in the Temple* (1669, National Museum, Stockholm), Rembrandt's only surviving son Titus died in 1668, and Titus's wife Magdelena gave birth to a daughter, Titia, in March 1669. Rembrandt himself was dying and he passed away in October 1669 and was buried in a pauper's grave. Magdalena, Titia's mother, died a few weeks later. This painting was found in Rembrandt's studio just after his death and is considered his last work, though unfinished.

The passage illustrated is from Luke's Gospel (2.21–35) which tells how the Holy Spirit had revealed to Simeon, a righteous man, that he would not die before the Messiah would come to Israel. Simeon was in the temple when Mary and Joseph brought Jesus there and he knew at that moment that Jesus was the promised Messiah. He took him in his arms and praised God saying: *Now dismiss your servant in peace. For my eyes have seen your salvation . . . a light for revelation to the Gentiles and for glory to your people Israel* (Luke 2:29–32). He blessed the child's parents, and said to Mary: *and a sword will pierce your own soul too.* These prophetic words to Mary were fulfilled at the crucifixion, and are the first words that point to the suffering that lay ahead for Jesus and his followers.

Rembrandt's painting focuses on Simeon's depth of emotion as he holds the Christ child. Only the shadowy face of a woman who may be the child's mother, or even the prophetess Anna, appears in the background. In the poem *Child in the Picture*, I reflect on the connection between Rembrandt and the old prophet Simeon, both awaiting their deaths, both rejoicing over new birth.

The birth of Titia must have been one bright moment in a world of sorrow for Rembrandt, and we can imagine Rembrandt nursing his grandchild, aware of his own failing health and imminent departure, thankful for this new life who was his present joy and the future hope for his family line. Perhaps it was the arrival of the new baby, Titia, who turned his thoughts to the coming of the Christ child as the subject of his last painting. He may have identified with Simeon who can depart in peace because in the Christ child he had seen *a light for revelation.* I wonder if it demonstrates Rembrandt's conviction that the huge volume of work he would leave would be an inspiration and light for the generations to come.

There is also the suggestion in the painting that a blessing, such as Simeon gave to the Christ-child, is desperately needed by his new-born grandchild Titia because of all that might lie ahead of her. He must have seen the great need for this fatherless, and soon-to-be motherless child, to receive the light of a heavenly Father's blessing. Perhaps his own last gift to her as he left this life, was to pronounce this blessing on her through his work of art.

Passing on the blessing

The blessing by Simeon is followed in Luke's Gospel by the account of the prophetess Anna giving thanks to God for the coming of the Christ child. She is like her namesake in the Old Testament, Hannah (both meaning *gracious*) who prayed in the temple, consecrating her son to the Lord, and giving thanks for the baby.

Simeon, in his blessing, takes up the words of the prophet Isaiah about the coming of the Servant of the Lord: *I will also make you a light for the Gentiles, that you may bring my salvation to the ends of the earth* (Isa 49:6). Jesus uses similar words to his disciples: *You are the light of the world* (Matt 5:14) and before he departed: *Go and make disciples of all nations* (Matt 28:19). In this way, Isaiah's prophetic words are passed on in the great commission of Jesus to his followers.

A further parallel is the blessing Jesus gave to children. Just as God's blessing was spoken by Simeon holding the Christ child in his arms, so too when mothers brought their children to Jesus, he took them in his arms and blessed them, to the surprise of the disciples who wanted to turn them away (Mark 10:13–16). The gospels emphasize that Jesus loves and welcomes children, and people of all ages who come to him with childlike faith, to be part of the family of God. To all who come, he passes on the blessing of love which he received from the Father.

What is more, having received God's blessing, he gives us the task of passing it on. The words of Jesus: *Whoever welcomes one of these little ones in my name, welcomes me . . . and the one who sent me* (Mark 9:37), was a challenge to the status-seeking disciples, and to us today, to see in every child and in the people considered of lowest rank, the presence of God himself, and to show respect and kindness to all.

I am grateful for the works of Rembrandt whose genius as an artist not only throws light on the complexity of human relationships and emotions, but also shows us how we are part of the picture.

9

Journey into Night

I will not live without love.

—Vincent Van Gogh, letter to Theo, 23 December 1882

JOURNEY INTO NIGHT

Silenced.
Only your worn suitcase tells your tale.
It weathered the journey with you. It held
your few possessions, your last thread of hope.
On its tough leather
you painted your name in bold.

Baying and stamping,
they hunted you like a fox
from the only place you knew as home.
Hounded across the river,
you were driven out, boxed in,
stricken with fear,

made dumb.
Like a sheep before shearers,
shorn of all you owned,
your little lambs torn from your arms
in the dead of night—
their cries ring out for ever in your ears.

Wheels grinding
they rounded you up, herded you
into trucks not fit for beasts,
trafficked you, thirst-ridden, shunted and jolted
on that long and calculated journey down the tracks
to the sinister site, wired and towered.

Brake-screech. End of the line.
Barking dogs, savagery.
Harsh commands, hurled out.
Smoke stench. Brutality.
Cruelty laboratory.
Blood flow on soil and snow.

Skin-and-bone, defenseless
branded, nameless,
clamped in sheds
in endless night,
lamp in the soul
snuffed out.

Finally, as precisely planned
in cold rage,
each playing his, her part,
they stifled
the breath of life in you,
silenced the beat of your heart,

flung your body, bruised and broken,
in the white-hot blaze,
dumped the smoldering ashes
of God's holy image
into the slime
of the fly-infested pond.

No stone or single plot of land
in memory.
No branch or tree.

Only an empty suitcase
with the dust of your dreams
bears your name, sounds it out
among so many, stored
and stacked like walls
whose very stones cry out.
Your coat, your shoes
are somewhere in those vast,
jumbled mounds.

And somewhere lost to you
in the seven-ton-mass of human hair,
ripped and knotted,
jet, bronze, fair and silver,
is the hair once blessed,
stroked and caressed

of your unique and splendid,
beautiful women and children
who loved you, honored you,
called you by name—

Lazarus Benjamin!

Name in bold letters
defies death and shame,
warning
his story
can happen again.

REFLECTION

The Jews of Krakow

Some events in history have had such repercussions for human existence that they must never be ignored or forgotten. An outstanding example is the holocaust. A recent visit to Krakow and the Auschwitz-Birkenau Memorial and Museum helped to give us a clearer picture of what happened at that time.

The old city center of Krakow has an impressive medieval Main Market Square with splendid historic buildings and the whole center is circled by a beautiful park. Set high on Wawel hill, overlooking the River Wisla, are Wawel Castle and Cathedral which date back to when Krakow was capital of Poland and the castle was the palace of the Polish kings. Just before the Nazi invasion in 1939, many of the castle treasures were taken secretly to Canada for safekeeping till after the war, and the castle became the headquarters of the Nazis. It is now a museum displaying the royal treasures.

Modern Krakow incorporates the Jewish quarter of Kazimierz, where the Jews settled after being expelled from Krakow at the close of the 15th century, and as time went on, they were joined by Jews from other countries who were fleeing persecution. Many of the newcomers were scholars and the area became renowned as a center for Jewish culture and education. We visited the Old Synagogue which houses the Judaic museum, and the 16th century Remuh synagogue with the adjoining Renaissance cemetery, with its Wailing Wall made from fragments of tombstones destroyed by the Nazis, as well as many ancient gravestones that were repaired after the desecration.

When the Nazis entered Krakow in the autumn of 1939, the population of Jews was recorded as nearly 70,000, amounting to around one quarter of Krakow's total inhabitants. They were immediately subjected to laws restricting their freedom and civil rights and made to wear yellow stars. Soon afterwards around 52,000 of these Jews were forced out of their homes for 'resettlement', deportation to labor camps in the east. The rest were allowed to stay as their presence was vital to the city's economy.

In spring 1941, the remaining Jewish community of around 18,000 from Kazimierz was given just a few days to leave their homes and were crowded into 320 buildings which had formerly housed 3000 people. This area was walled off as a ghetto with its gates under armed guard. Those who were able were subjected to forced labor in factories, such as Oscar Schindler's Enamel Factory. The rest were soon transported in groups of thousands to Auschwitz.

The Ghetto Heroes Square which marks the center of the Podgorze ghetto is on the other side of the River Wisla to Kazimierz. It is empty except for seventy chairs of iron and bronze arranged randomly, representing the loss of all those thousands of people who were executed on the spot or deported for extermination. Nearby, outside the Oscar Schindler Factory Museum, is another chair representing the 1,200 Jews that Schindler saved. Schindler's Factory today houses a very moving and informative exhibition on the Nazi occupation of Krakow.

Many brave Polish individuals and members of the Resistance assisted the Jews in the ghetto by obtaining false travel documents or vital supplies like medicine. One of these was the pharmacist Tadeusz Pankiewicz, who chose to remain in the ghetto quarter in order to rescue Jews. His pharmacy is now the Museum of National Remembrance in Ghetto Heroes Square.

Auschwitz-Birkenau

Walking through these parts of the city helped to create a context for a trip from Krakow to Auschwitz-Birkenau, one of a huge network of camps built by the Nazis to annihilate Jews from all over Europe. One million of the 1.1 million people transported to Auschwitz were Jews, but there was also a large group of non-Jewish Poles as part of the Nazi policy of liquidating the Poles to make room for German resettlement. The main targets were the educated people or anyone with high social status, as well as mass killings of the disabled or chronically ill, people deemed "unworthy of life." Gypsy populations, homosexuals and Jehovah's Witnesses, pacifists who refused to do military service or work in arms factories, and captured Soviets suffered the same fate. It is estimated that in total the people all across Europe murdered by the Nazis amounted to 17 million.

Stepping into the death camp under the archway with the inscription *Arbeit Macht Frei,* we found the prison cells, the cells where the Franciscan priest Kolbe took the place of a prisoner for execution, the room for Mengele's medical experimentation, the black wall for shootings, the chambers for Zyclon B poison gas, and the crematoria. There were also the rooms piled high with victims' belongings, the ones that their torturers had no time to destroy.

Visitors, crowds of all ages and nationalities, were leaving in subdued silence. I saw one man in deep distress, others comforting him. I felt chilled and shocked, yet somehow the voice of a human spirit, a branded person whose every aspect of life had been violated, rose above the stark surroundings and communicated. He was one person from a whole population systematically targeted, disempowered, demeaned, reduced to an object, a name lost among the records the Nazis managed to destroy when the camp was liberated. In my poem *Journey into Night* I think of him.

The visit for me was a disturbing reminder of the importance in our own times of standing against all forms of Neo-Nazi ideology, with its blatant intolerance of racial differences, the sense of national superiority and rejection of international links and ties, the spread of propaganda through social media, the contempt shown towards those who express an alternative viewpoint or moral conscience, the denial of dignity to the weak, disabled, or any minority group, and the tendency to blame these groups for the evils or failures in our society. If the opposite of love is not hate but indifference, as holocaust survivor, Elie Wiesel said in an interview after receiving the 1986 Nobel Peace Prize, we might ask ourselves how our own attitudes towards any minority group measure up today.

A visit to the death camp defies description. Unspeakable was the first word to come to mind. Yet we are urged to speak out for voices that have been silenced. Some did write and their poetry survived them, like the Jewish Hungarian poet and academic, Miklós Radnóti who wrote his Postcard poems on the long march from the Bor concentration camp in what is now Serbia in 1944 when he was just 35 years old. Beaten because he was writing, then shot with others who had been made too weak to walk, and buried in a mass grave, his little notebook was found when his body was exhumed years later by his family.

Night

Probably the most famous and powerful memoir from the holocaust is *Night* by Elie Wiesel, about his experience in Buchenwald when he was only fifteen. Although I read it many years ago, its impact is unforgettable. Translated into some 35 different languages, it is one of more than 40 books written by Wiesel. In *Night*, he describes his first night in Auschwitz in chilling words, with the seven-times repeated phrase, "Never shall I forget."

Journey into Night is the result of my struggle to find words after my visit to Auschwitz-Birkenau. It is a reflection on the loss of one precious human being, the waste of his gift to mankind. He was perhaps one of the many talented people who despite being deprived of everything, managed to maintain elements of their rich cultural life while in the Krakow ghetto. I wanted to honor one person who had written his name on his suitcase so it wouldn't be lost and articulate his message of Shalom when he could not. For me, he is a representative of the millions who suffered the same fate.

The powerful documentary, *Night Will Fall*, made from footage of the release of prisoners from death camps, was produced by Sidney Bernstein in 1945 and released on the 70th anniversary of the event. The title is taken from the warning in the film's commentary that if the world doesn't learn the lesson that the pictures teach, night will fall.

The deliberate murder of children by the Nazis as part of their attempt to eliminate the Jews is the darkest part of the whole incomprehensible history of the holocaust. I'll never forget finding upstairs in the Pinkas Synagogue in Prague, the exhibition of paintings by Jewish children who were transported to the Terezin ghetto prison camp in 1942. They were taught secretly by their art teacher Friedl Dicker-Brandeis, a versatile artist who had studied under Paul Klee in Germany. An Austrian Jew, she fled to Prague and worked in theatre design as well as teaching. She brought her materials with her to Terazin ghetto and used her theatre techniques there with the children so that they could enjoy performing.

Using progressive teaching methods, she encouraged her pupils to express their thoughts and feelings through painting. Just before the occupants of Terezin were all transported to Auschwitz, Friedl gathered all 4,500 paintings, each with the child's name, and hid them in two suitcases. When discovered at the end of the war, they were given to the synagogue. All that is left of those children's lives is that collection of pictures. They were all gassed along with their teacher and most of their parents.

Heeding the warnings

The aim of the Auschwitz-Birkenau Memorial and Museum is to preserve the historic site, its hundreds of buildings, and thousands of artefacts and documents, in order to save the memory of the lives lost in the holocaust. Through the evidence the site provides, it is hoped that visitors and study groups will resolve to build a safer, more peaceful world, or in the words of the president of the memorial museum, Dr Piotre Cywinski, the aim is "to warn humanity against itself." He also emphasizes that the goal of education about the Holocaust is not only to learn facts from the past, but also to see how they link with today's threats and challenges, and to take active responsibility for our contemporary world.

When we make choices, as Wiesel says, there is no neutral ground. One thing the holocaust event, archetype of evil, demonstrates is that ordinary people who take one step of acquiescence along the path of oppression could contribute to power structures tightening their grip on the defenseless, and from there taking hold of society.

As national governments become increasingly intolerant of minority faith groups, we see levels of religious persecution rising in many countries throughout the world, with Open Doors estimating as many as 245 million Christians worldwide facing high levels of persecution in more than 70 countries. In parts of the Middle East there has been a genocide of the Christian population. Many other religious people groups, like the Uighurs in China, suffer severe persecution. At the same time, the Jewish populations across the globe are suffering the greatest rise in anti-Semitism since the war. The Memorial at Auschwitz-Birkenau is a timely reminder for all to speak out against evil and injustice. As Elie Wiesel writes in *Night*, there is a response in responsibility. We are all called to put our memorial and our protest into words and actions.

10

Moments in Israel

He who loves much does much, and is capable of much, and that which is done with love is well done.
—VINCENT VAN GOGH, LETTER TO THEO, 3 APRIL 1878

DOMINUS FLEVIT

Moan with the Dome
at the dawn call to prayer
Knell with the bell
of the Holy Sepulchre
Whine as the sirens
of patrol cars blare

As sons of the prophets mourn
wail by the Wall
As Peter wept at cock-crow
remembering Christ's call
in deep sorrow
weep

As the mother hen
grieves for her children
who forsake
her sheltering wings
the Son of Man weeps

As Rachel weeping for her children
women of Jerusalem
let your tears
pour on his feet
he will wash yours

Let his voice
speak in your ear
at the empty tomb
Rejoice!
(Your name is on his lips)
Noli timere
Do not fear.

SONG AT THE DOME AND THE POOL

A single phrase of song I sing
    like a feather floating
        upward, meandering

now a dove's wing
    bearing a message
        soaring, spiraling

tracing the arcs
    of the giant dome
        then returning

a flurry of doves
    dipping, quivering,
        glistening like falling snow.

Echoes of song
    a pattern imprinting
        ice-flakes on my sun-burnt skin.

Beneath in the hewn rock
of the ancient healing pool
myself I bring

and watch
the water tremble
concentric circles
ring upon ring

released
by a single
touch.

Eyes opened
ears unstopped
the lame leap like deer
the mute tongue shouts for joy
joy upon joy.

LAKE WATER

Snows of Hermon
springs of Dan
streams of Jordan
flow through you
fish and fly breed in you
blood has been spilled in you

patriot and pilgrim
politician and preacher
sport on you
strive for you
contemplate you
debate you

while I in a wooden boat
float on you
on the rainbow lights of Tiberius
and the moon's arc
which glow on you
a cool night breeze blows on you
like a breath

a voice from your shore
calling to the figure
in the fisherman's cowl
who leaps out
naked-faith
into your chill water

MASADA

Dead Sea
bronze mirror
to a saffron sky

Rising sun
the waking eye
watchful, viewing
mountain sands
veiled in ghostly
violet gowns

High on fortress stone
we stand
on dust that mixes
earth with bone
the salt and grit
of human valor

We gaze on this
the first we've known
of desert grandeur

and history's toxic chamber.

TREE OF LIFE

Under the waving fronds
stripped from stately palms
by chanting throngs,
Messiah chose to ride
through the city's Golden Gate
to the grief inside.

Under the outstretched vine
where fruit was gathered and trampled
for Passover wine,
Yeshua chose to declare
that branches joined to him
his root would share.

Under the ancient olive
where fruit was plucked and crushed
for temple oil,
the Anointed chose to pray
as in the depths of night
he was betrayed.

Under the thorn-spiked crown,
torn from the thirsty earth
and sin-cursed ground,
the Son chose forgiveness
to plant the tree of life
in all its fullness.

Under the apple blossom
where rising sap of spring
awakes a garden,
I celebrate,
a seed of earth the King of Heaven
chose to recreate.

CHOICE

I choose to follow
in the way of the cross of Jesus,
the path of humility and service;
I lay my sin and sorrow,
time and talents
at his feet.

I choose to declare
that I am a part of Christ the vine,
joined with all branches of believers
who bear the fruit of the Spirit,
God's loving presence
dwelling within us.

I choose to pray
Father, your will be done;
even in the darkest hour,
the toughest times
I will trust you, place my fears
into your hands.

I choose to forgive
all those who've hurt me
or accused me falsely,
undervalued me or scorned me.
I release each one by the power of the Spirit
who sets our hearts free.

I choose to live,
rise from the tomb of disbelief,
guilt and disappointment,
step into the light of Christ
who died and rose again to rescue me.
I choose the gift of freedom, hope, and love.

REFLECTION

A place of pilgrimage

Israel, an historic trade route for travelers from Asia, Europe and Africa, has also long been the sacred destination for pilgrims from the three monotheistic faiths, Jews, Christians, and Muslims. Seeing the connections of actual places with the Biblical accounts of the events in Jesus's life, as well as those linked with the Old Testament narrative, gave us a much better visual understanding of the Bible and its history.

Arriving in the Old City, we soon saw reminders of the long, troubled history of Jerusalem, a name which ironically means city of peace. There are seven gates, each leading to a distinct part of the city, except the Eastern or Golden gate that was walled off by the sultans. The Eastern gate is mentioned in Ezekiel's prophecy as the one through which the prince would enter (Ezek 44:1–3). It faces the road to the Mount of Olives and so it's considered to be the gate Jesus Messiah took on Palm Sunday as he entered Jerusalem on his way to the Temple, as I allude to in the poem *Tree of Life*. There, in the Temple, he met people buying and selling in preparation for the Passover feast and Jesus told them, quoting the prophets: *My house will be called a house of prayer for all nations,* whereas they had made it *a den of robbers* (Mark 11:17; Isa 56:7; Jer 7:11).

The Western Wall is a surviving piece of the Temple Mount, most sacred because it is nearest to the Holy of Holies, the innermost sanctuary. Because this fragment of wall is all that remains of the temple destroyed by the Romans a few decades after Jesus's lifetime, and has survived the many sieges and bombardments since, it has become a symbol of the endurance of the Jewish people themselves. They look to the covenant God made with Abraham that the land he would give to Abraham and Sarah's descendants would be their everlasting inheritance (Gen 17:7–8). Jews all over the world pray facing this wall, also known as the Wailing Wall because through the ages Jewish pilgrims have gone there to cry out to God for the rebuilding of the Jerusalem Temple. Nowadays, people of all faiths place written prayers in the wall's crevices and they are collected twice yearly by a Rabbi and buried in the cemetery on the Mount of Olives. This reflects the original ethos of the temple referred to in Isaiah as *a house of prayer for all nations.*

For all nations

Many churches are built on sites associated with events in the life of Jesus, sometimes over ancient crypts that connect layers of history and tradition. The Church of the Holy Sepulchre, shared by six distinct Christian traditions, is regarded as the holiest site because of early excavations uncovering what are thought to be the rock of Golgotha and the tomb of Christ.

The Church of the Pater Noster on the Mount of Olives is built on the site of a cave long associated with Jesus's teaching on prayer. We were fascinated by the decorative ceramic plaques on the walls, each with the *Our Father* prayer written in one of 140 different languages.

Also, on the slopes of the Mount of Olives in the Garden of Gethsemane is the Church of All Nations, with decorations from the sixteen nations who contributed to its construction. On the front tympanum is a mosaic illustrating Jesus as the "link between God and the human race."

I especially liked the brightly colored mosaic paintings on the walls of the Church of the Annunciation in Nazareth that depict mother and child through the eyes of artists from forty-three nations. It is another reminder of Jesus's words that what we do for others we do for him. In these pictures every child is Jesus, the child of Vietnam, Thailand, Korea, Japan, China, and many others. They also all represent the children Jesus said would be in his kingdom. It is a celebration of Jesus coming as the light of the whole world.

The church, whose name I've taken as the title for my poem *Dominus Flevit*, is built on the site of a fifth century Byzantine monastery on the slopes of the Mount of Olives. The modern church is constructed in the shape of a tear drop in memory of the Lord who wept as he looked down on Jerusalem and foretold its destruction with the words, *If you had only known on this day what would bring you peace* (Luke 19.41–44). Jesus wept like Isaiah the prophet who cried, *let me weep bitterly . . . over the destruction of my people* (Isa 22:4).

Jesus had earlier expressed great sorrow over Jerusalem: *O Jerusalem, Jerusalem . . . how often I have longed to gather your children together, as a hen gathers her chick under her wings, but you were not willing* (Luke13:34–35). The same utterance was spoken again on the Tuesday of Passion Week (Matt 23:37–39). Here Christ was using an image familiar to the Jews, the wings of a mother bird guarding her young, representing the refuge and shelter offered by God himself (Ps 57:1; 61:4). Both these gospel passages end in a positive note, pointing to a time when Jesus will return and the people of Jerusalem will say, *Blessed is he who comes in the name of the Lord.*

Dominus Flevit is also a reminder of the tears Jesus shed with Mary and the mourners when Lazarus had died. When they saw Jesus weep, the mourners commented: *See how he loved him* (John 11:35–36). At the time, Jesus was facing his own impending death and in identifying with these mourners, perhaps he was also empathizing with the pain and sorrow his followers would soon experience. To all who have followed since, this example of Jesus weeping with those who weep, offers comfort.

Women affirmed

Various gospel accounts, such as Jesus weeping with Mary at the grave of Lazarus, appreciating her devotion when she washed and anointed his feet, addressing Mary Magdalene by name as she wept by the tomb, and appearing to the group of women who'd come to the empty tomb, bidding them to rejoice and not be afraid (Matt 28:9–10), are among the many striking examples in the Gospels that show Jesus's attitude to women. He was sensitive to their emotions, defending them when others were quick to judge, honoring them by appearing to them first after his resurrection and giving them the task of telling the good news to the male disciples.

Jesus lifted the status of women in a society where they were expected to keep to domestic duties, by commending Mary of Bethany for sitting at his feet as the other disciples would do, even though sitting at a rabbi's feet was regarded as a privilege reserved for men. (Michele Guinness, *Woman, the Full Story*, Zondervan, 2003, p.116).

Although these are incidents in Christ's life either alluded to or simply present in my mind as I wrote *Dominus Flevit*, at its heart is my own encounter with the Jesus of the Gospels, meeting in faith the compassionate, ever-present One, who knows our heartaches and heals our brokenness. No matter what sorrow life brings, he has suffered before us and his resurrection life is the gift he has for us in every situation.

Song at the Dome and the Pool was inspired by St Anne's Church and the Pool of Bethesda. St Anne's is one of the oldest preserved churches, built over a crypt honoring the birthplace of Mary. From early times it was thought to be the site of the home of St Anne, mentioned in a second century apocryphal scripture as mother of Mary and grandmother of Jesus. It is one of the few Crusader churches not destroyed by Saladin's conquest in 1187 but spared to become a Madrasa until its later restoration as a church. When we entered, it must have been early morning because no one else was there, and when I looked up into the dome, I instinctively began to sing a few notes. I was immediately astonished by the echoing sound, and it wasn't until years later that I discovered that the church is well known for its acoustics and is the favorite venue for many famous soloists and choirs.

St. Anne's is situated just inside Lions' Gate, formerly known as Sheep Gate, and beside the Pool of Bethesda, an extensive archeological site where colonnades can be seen. These are mentioned in the Biblical account of the Pool of Bethesda where Christ healed a man who had been an invalid for 38 years. He'd been waiting such a long time, he told Jesus, for someone to help him to get into the pool when the waters were stirred (John 5:2–8). It was a pool known for its medicinal properties but the action of Jesus showed that he himself was the true healing pool, the Messiah foretold by the prophets: *Then will the eyes of the blind be opened and the ears of the deaf unstopped. Then will the lame leap like a deer, and the mute tongue shout for joy* (Isa 35:5–6).

Natural features

The physical features of desert, river, springs, lakes and hillsides, as well as the plants and trees in Israel, are often reminders of biblical events and symbols.

Lake Water recalls our trip on an old-style wooden boat on the Sea of Galilee one evening. It reminded me of the last account of Jesus at the lake, when his disciples had been fishing all night and caught nothing (John 21). Jesus, appearing after his resurrection, called to them from the shore and told them to cast their nets on the other side, whereupon their nets were filled to breaking point. When John said to Peter, "It is the Lord!," Peter immediately swam ashore to meet Jesus, the others following with the catch. His spontaneous action was an indication of his faith, joy, and eagerness to meet with Jesus, and is a challenge to share his response.

When they came ashore, Jesus had lit a fire for a bread and fish breakfast. Recalling Peter's bitter tears after his threefold denial, he asked Peter if he had agape love for him, the unconditional love that Jesus had shown to all those in need. He then gave Peter the responsibility that was his own during his lifetime, of caring for and feeding the sheep. The disciples were to follow Christ's way of sacrificial leadership, and for Peter and the others, this would mean laying down their lives. My trip on the lake, so familiar to those fishermen, reminded me of the cost of discipleship and the sacrifice being made by so many followers of Christ who are persecuted in countries around the world today.

Our dawn climb up the sandy, table mountain fortress of Masada where families of the Jewish resistance forces took refuge after the fall of Jerusalem, prompted me to write my impressions in *Masada*. The site of the Roman siege in the surroundings of the desert, and the resulting death to suicide of so many trapped within, as described by the historian Josephus, is another terrible reminder of human oppression.

The poem *Tree of Life*, links trees and shrubs that we saw around Jerusalem with the events leading up to the death of Christ. I reflect on the impact of seeing these plants growing and on the wider symbolism.

Along a path from the southern wall of old Jerusalem, near the excavation site of the City of David, we came across a vine that formed a canopy over an entire seating area used as a cafe. As it was the Sabbath day, the cafe was empty and the whole area quiet. We sat for some time looking up at the spreading branches, heavily laden with bunches of grapes above us. I imagined Jesus seated under a vine like this when he taught his disciples, all of them very aware that the vineyard was an Old Testament symbol of Israel. This gave the words Jesus used about himself an added depth of meaning: *I am the vine; you are the branches . . . apart from me you can do nothing* (John 15:5). I pictured the disciples reaching and eating the grapes, listening as Jesus promised to those who remained in him, lives that produced fruit, a consequence of the life he shared with them. It was a reminder too of the little group gathered later with Jesus, sharing the last Passover supper, drinking the fruit of the vine together just before he died. It was then that Jesus established the wine as a symbol of his life blood poured out in death for them and for the sins of the world (Luke 22:16–20).

The fruitful palm, indicating an oasis in the desert and a joy to the traveler, is a symbol of life and blessing in the Bible: *The righteous will flourish like a palm tree . . . They will still bear fruit in old age, they will stay fresh and green* (Ps 92:12–15). Its motif was carved on the temple walls and on the doors of the inner sanctuary as a sign of praise and blessing, and its leaves were carried and waved with songs of praise at the feasts and ceremonies of ancient Israel, as in *Blessed is he who comes in the name of the Lord* (Ps 118:26–27). These were the words of praise that the crowds took up, waving palm branches as Jesus entered Jerusalem (Mark 11:8–10). Sadly, the common date palm, due to infestation of weevil, is rapidly declining in Israel today.

The olive, most common tree of Israel and a present-day symbol of the nation, also represents blessing in the Bible: *But I am like an olive tree flourishing in the house of God; I trust in God's unfailing love for ever and ever* (Ps 52:8). When we went to the Garden of Gethsemane, which means oil press, we saw olive trees that have been carbon dated to nearly a thousand years old. Olive trees if cut down can spring back from shoots of a root, so these may well be offshoots of ones that sheltered Jesus when he prayed in the darkness of the garden (Matt 26:36–46).

On the Mount of Olives we noticed many thorny shrubs like huge thistles. They reminded me of the crown placed on Jesus in mockery by the Roman soldiers who crucified him, and of the ground cursed with thorns and thistles in the Genesis story when mankind sinned.

In the fifth verse of the poem *Tree of Life*, the apple tree represents home in Ireland and personal spiritual resurrection. After my visit I planted an apple tree in my garden, and every spring its blossom reminds me of life that we enjoy now in Christ, and will be complete in a new body on God's new earth. *Choice* is a reflective response to the choices Jesus made, described in my poem *Tree of Life*.

The tree of life

The Bible begins with the picture of the tree of life in the Garden of Eden, representing immortality in paradise which was lost through sin, and closes with the vision of the river in the heavenly Eden with its tree of life for the healing of the nations. Between the two is the tree on which Christ died and the garden of his resurrection. By his death and resurrection, Jesus took the curse of sin and death that all humans experience, replacing it with blessing and life to all who believe. As he himself taught, *I have come in order that you might have life — life in all its fullness* (John 10:10). The tree of life is ultimately a symbol of Jesus himself, as well as a symbol of his followers bearing the fruit of his Spirit in their lives in every part of the earth.

A visit to Israel inevitably makes us very conscious of so much conflict in that region throughout history. Today as never before, we need to heed the words of the Psalmist: *Pray for the peace of Jerusalem: May those who love you be secure* (Ps 122:6).

11

Consider the Lilies

It's good to love flowers and pine branches and ivy and hedges of hawthorn, we have seen them from the very beginning.
—Vincent Van Gogh, letter to Theo, 23 March 1877

MOMENTS OF WONDER IN A GARDEN

1.

Relax. Enjoy.
Today is not a day to cut the grass
or wonder why it grows so fast
or why the weeds aren't chosen fodder
for snail or slug or caterpillar.

I watch wing-shadows dive and glide
across the sunlit green—
from overhead a shadow theater—
birds that swoop and disappear.
At my feet the flourishing clover
is sweet to bumblebees that hover
and a butterfly dancing, cream silk kimono,
on the leaf-hand of a Japanese Acer.

Milk-white blooms of lilac in May
turned to cones of parchment,
I snipped and gathered them only yesterday.
Now is the time for orange blossom,
(Philadelphus, love for brother)
its snowy clusters, a constellation of stars,
freshness of heaven birthed
from deep and hidden roots
in earth.

2.

Only human travel paths leave trails of smoke;
as I look up, planes, mosquito-like,
scrawl tags of white graffiti
across the sunlit blue
and I wonder at the frequency, incessancy of flight,

the rumble and grind of engines.
Then as I listen—
the branches' persistent motion,
their whisper,
conversation in the breeze,

and from sycamore, spruce and ash,
the rambling fuchsia with its fiery spray of bells—
the harmony of so many birds this morning,
voices ringing out
and tuning in to one another,

chime and trill and chatter
rhythms of family, foraging and food,
rhyme of an earth,
for the time being,
still good.

3.

In warmth like this so rare on Emerald Isle
we greet and smile,
remark with wonder, note with praise;
forgive that I forget on cold, wet days

that rain too is a gift so often craved—
its pouring streams that filter deep with surging springs,
the hope of wells from hidden chambers of the earth—
the cry of hearts in many a parched land.

4.

Fruit trees and bushes
I planted long ago and seldom tend
are necklaced with green beads,
promises hidden in bunches,
hard, bright gems.

The wonder is, despite my lack of care,
soon they'll plump and ooze
blackcurrant extravagance,
red-apple exuberance,
the glut and indulgence of rich purple plum,

juices spurting, staining the tongue,
the squelch and drizzle
of fruit fallen,
decay and seed in abundance
pungently seeping the earth.

5.

Life-giving Spirit in this place,
root of all knowledge, wise and true,
seed of hope, buried, raised,
source of harmony, bounty and grace,

as I turn to the soil to dig and weed,
I turn to you to fill and feed
this thirsty heart, this earth, our world,
each moment of wonder
with you.

PRODIGALS' CONFESSION

You gave us a spring, a sparkling stream
We built a mill, an acid spill
We thirst, our hands unclean.

You gave us a fold, a field of green
We built high towers and tore down trees
We've wounded the land and our souls.

You gave us a deep and healing pool
We trust big brands that span the globe
We set our hearts on stone.

You offered us life, our daily bread
We feed on offers of gold instead
We hunger, hunger for more.

You opened a door, you shone a light
We built a prison with carbon emissions
We tremble, we're trapped inside.

You gave us an inheritance
It's spent
We thought the party wouldn't end.

You offered wine
We cursed the vine
And all the while we've played at let's pretend.

WHALE INSTINCTS

Today I discovered my affinity
to the toothed whales:
the killer, the short-finned pilot,
the narwhal and beluga

and that I'm part of their select community
of female mammals
who, in a post reproductive lifespan,
care for grandchildren.

After all this time,
the wisdom of the whale instinct uncovered,
their family bonds
and evolutionary purposes,

diving deep
beneath blue ocean surfaces
to secure the survival
of the young.

WHO DO YOU THINK YOU ARE?

In China where ancestors are honored
you were the Emperor's
prized possession
given equal status
with his wives

with your own little palace,
private servants, armed guard,
fed with delicacies,
showed off
to all important friends

who admired you,
took you to their kingdoms,
Korea, Thailand and Japan.
In Tibet they made you
guardian of temples.

Transported on trade ships,
you were the fashionable guest
in royal courts of Europe.
Italy gave you a carriage and costume,
your own little feathered cap.

In London, Victoria, Empress of India,
pampered you on her velvet couch,
sipping tea from her china cup.
You were her Olga, Pedro, Minka,
Fatima, Venus and Mops.

An author snubbed you—
no sporting prowess,
no useful purpose,
but to people who knew you better
you were charming,

strong-willed
but certainly not pugnacious.
When you featured on an ad
for a Vodafone launch
the whole of India wanted you.

So tonight, Corah, as he lies
curled up on your duvet
with one eye open on his wrinkly face
watching you,
tell him his bedtime story,

the true tale, that he is the oldest,
most highly revered
of all canine breeds on the planet,
and 2,500 years ago,
applauded by wise Confucius.

Tell him proudly
that the Romans said
he's a lot of dog in a small space.
He'll raise one brow
in a quizzical look,

then nod off in beautiful dreams
of Lion Dog ancestors
and the Pekingese
on a plush velvet throne
with a silken rug,

a golden dish with a chunky stew
served up for the honorable,
royal, adorable
Gizmo,
your unsurpassable pug.

CONSIDER THE LILIES

A few fragile lilies arrayed
in a glass jar
their sunshine yellow
warming the white and silver
of your small ward
in November
the last time I saw you.

Before they fade
their image you save
in vivid pastels—
the last picture you made.

Though lilies in their glory fall
your gift of courage
still will flourish,
framed on my memory,
ablaze on my wall.

ROCK AMONG WILD GRASS

Rock
among
the wild grass
Foothold
on the cliff path
Strong while flowers wilt and fall
Seat of rest for those who pass
Jacob's pillow—
Angel vision
Bethel's pillar—
Gate of heaven
Bedrock, ground for daily living
Mighty Rock of all.

REFLECTION

Contemplation

The current focus on mental health and finding ways to a calm and peaceful frame of mind is central to the teaching of Jesus in the gospels and has longstanding Jewish roots. The prophet Isaiah speaks of the peace of mind that comes from a moment-by-moment trust in God: *You will keep in perfect peace those whose minds are steadfast, because they trust in you* (Isa 26:3).

There is a long history of contemplative practices in the faith traditions of Jews and Christians. Doug Oman writes about four key practices in contemplation common to traditions of all origins: setting aside specific time, centering oneself at times throughout the day, emphasizing personal character growth, and drawing inspiration from spiritual models. As Oman explains, the integration of these practices needs to be based on a valid, coherent worldview (*Contemplative Practices in Action*, ed. Thomas Plante, Praeger, 2010, pp.12–13). A Christian worldview, founded on the love of God in Christ, is the clear message of the New Testament and the starting point for finding peace and wisdom in our daily lives.

Jesus reflected on the beauty of nature when teaching about trusting God rather than living with anxiety: *Consider the lilies, how they grow; they neither toil nor spin; yet I tell you, even Solomon in all his glory was not arrayed like one of these.* (Luke 12:27 RSV). He also showed by example the importance of finding a quiet space to commune with God, for he often rose early before the crowds came, and went outdoors to pray.

Thankfulness with prayer helps us overcome anxiety: *Do not be anxious about anything, but in everything, by prayer and petition, with thanksgiving, present your requests to God* (Phil 4:6). Only faith in the loving kindness and goodness of God makes it possible to live the way Paul recommends: *Be joyful always, pray continually, give thanks in all circumstances, for this is God's will for you in Christ Jesus* (1Thess 5: 16–18). I believe that prayer is essentially God reaching out to us in love and our trusting, thankful response.

To pray with another person is to help them be aware of God's presence so they can hear him speak his word within them.

Meditation with thankfulness for the glory and goodness of God revealed in nature is a frequent theme of the Psalms. At the end of a magnificent song of praise to God for all of creation, the Psalmist writes: *May my meditation be pleasing to him, as I rejoice in the Lord* (Ps 104:34).

This is in keeping with modern psychology's emphasis on the power of expressing gratitude, which some studies have shown can lead to increased awareness, a greater sense of optimism, self-confidence, better sleep patterns, relief of stress, with resulting physical and social benefits. Some research has claimed that gratitude even helps to rewire anxious pathways in the brain. It seems clear there are blessings for people who are generous with praise.

Healing power of nature

Moments of Wonder in a Garden resulted from tuning my senses to being consciously aware of all that I saw around me one morning in the garden. I find that practicing awareness of surroundings helps me to appreciate both the gift of nature and the gift of people whom we meet casually from day to day. It moves my focus from anxious thoughts to awareness of God's presence in all things.

The joy and spiritual blessing of gardens became especially apparent to me when we went one spring to Japan to work at the Christian University of Kwansei Gakuin, not far from Osaka. We visited ancient palaces and temples set in beautiful gardens, like the ones in Kyoto which we saw when irises were blooming by the ponds and streams, with their bridges and stepping stones. Although we were in Japan when my daughter was just a child, the experience had a profound effect on her. She has always remembered the crafts she learned there, origami, flower arranging and making sushi. When we moved to our present home, the first plants I put in our garden were the shrubs and trees I saw in small home gardens all around us in Nishinomiya that spring, flowering cherry, magnolia and camellia.

The healing properties of nature have long been extolled in Japan, and exercise in forest areas (forest bathing) is advocated as part of the national health program to counter the effects of stress. Recent studies in the west have shown that patients with a room with a view are less depressed and heal faster, and children are calmer in classrooms that face natural green areas.

Opportunity to appreciate the natural world is often a luxury outside the experience of many families, such as those who live in urban or rural poverty. As a student I shared a room with a Ugandan girl whom I took for a visit to the mountains. She viewed the landscape and said that for her, rather than being beautiful, mountains were an acute reminder of her mother's life spent in back-breaking drudgery, digging on the mountain slopes of her home near Kabale. To millions of others, whose lives are blighted by the effects of pollution and global warming, drought, fire, famine or flooding, or by the brutality of war, beauty is the next plate of food, access to fresh water or a roof over their heads.

Caring for the environment

In December 2018, David Attenborough, the naturalist and film-maker, gave a speech at the United Nations Climate Summit in Katowice, Poland. He told the representatives from almost 200 nations: "Right now, we're facing a man-made disaster of global scale, our greatest threat in thousands of years: climate change. If we don't take action, the collapse of our civilizations and the extinction of much of the natural world is on the horizon." Accompanying Attenborough's speech was footage of people standing in front of the remains of their homes incinerated by wildfires.

The following day at the same conference, the fifteen-year-old Swedish girl, Greta Thunberg, who had started widespread demonstrations among school children a few months before, gave her presentation about the danger of extinction.

In May 2019, there was a further warning: a UN report by biodiversity experts into the impact of humans on nature showed that nearly one million species, 25% of all flora and fauna on earth, are at risk of becoming extinct within decades, unless radical action is taken.

If we believe as the Psalmist writes, *the heavens declare the glory of God; the skies proclaim the work of his hands. Day after day they pour forth speech . . . Their voice goes out into all the earth, their words to the ends of the world* (Ps 19:1–4), then the way we use our natural environment is not just a political and moral issue. It's an issue of how we enable people to hear what the heavens are declaring about God. We need to ask how by our lifestyles we can help, not just ourselves, but all of earth's inhabitants, to experience the beauty and goodness of God in nature and the environment. Destruction and exploitation, resulting in suffering and death, point to forces of evil and greed in the world, and hide the glory of God.

The first sin of mankind described as taking the forbidden fruit in the Genesis story, has clear parallels with present day problems of exploitation of the environment and fellow human beings for personal and corporate gain. Because of widespread disregard, ignorance or deliberate repudiation of God's commandments, our world has suffered the loss of its moral compass just as described in the Biblical Eden.

In his documentary *Charles Darwin and the Tree of Life*, referring to the Biblical account of God instructing Adam and Eve to subdue the earth and have dominion over the creatures in it, David Attenborough complained that "that passage in Genesis gives humanity permission to exploit the natural world as they wish."

However, this mandate given by God in Genesis has in fact the opposite meaning. The Judeo-Christian belief is that God gave mankind responsibility for the environment, to be a protector and not an abuser of the natural world. The permission to rule given to humanity was in the context of people being obedient to God's rule as king. The first chapter of Genesis shows that all aspects of creation have close interdependence and harmony, because God made them and saw them as good. Regard for the interdependence of all forms of life is a Biblical principle that should govern any management of the environment. As the Christian Declaration on Nature drawn up at Assisi in 1986 insists, any exploitation of the earth, its creatures and its resources, is a denial of God and his love for the earth.

The misuse of the natural environment is the focus of my poem, *Prodigals' Confession*. In Jesus's parable, the prodigal son squanders his inheritance by his materialistic and wasteful lifestyle until, having lost everything, he returns to ask his father's forgiveness. The images in the poem also relate to Christ's words about living water, bread of life, light for the world, the true vine and the shepherd and sheepfold.

The films by David Attenborough and other wildlife photographers provide us with amazing footage of a multitude of creatures sharing our planet. We are constantly gaining new information about the variety of forms of animal life, their social interactions, emotional responses and intelligence. I wrote *Whale Instincts* on hearing of a recent discovery about the behavior of some whale communities.

Many young children have a spontaneous interest in animals, but some have a particularly close connection. Our granddaughter, Corah, shares a love for animals with her dad and so I've written about her beloved pet in *Who do you think you are?* Corah is a unique character, fun-loving and compassionate like her dad, and Paul's love and commitment to his daughter has made us proud of all that he has achieved as a father.

The new earth

Consider the Lilies is a tribute to Dave McClenaghan, a teacher of environmental studies, amateur musician and artist, keen cyclist, and above all, a compassionate family man. After his death from cancer, his wife Eileen brought me as a gift the last picture he painted in hospital while he was physically very weak yet strong in spirit. She raised her four children, the youngest having Down's Syndrome and acute health needs, with faith, strength and commitment. Her life is a real inspiration to me and many others.

Christ taught that one day He will return to earth. Then the *new heaven and a new earth* will be established (Isa 65:17, Rev 21:1, 4). *There will be no more death or mourning . . . for the old order of things has passed away.* Caring for the environment is of vital importance in the life-giving kingdom work of the church in the world, involving transformation not only of individual lives, but of structures and societies.

It is the Christian calling and privilege to contribute to the ultimate goal of human history described in the Bible, the time when creation will be completely renewed with the coming of Jesus as king to restore all things. We are to be a light of hope in the world. St. Paul writes, *I consider that our present sufferings are not worth comparing with the glory that will be revealed in us. The creation waits in eager expectation for the sons of God to be revealed . . . in hope that the creation itself will be liberated from its bondage to decay and brought into the glorious freedom of the children of God* (Rom 8:18–21).

Rock Among Wild Grass takes me back to a path on the north coast of Ireland, the same shore where, after a run on the beach, I wrote the first poem in this book. Along this path, I rested on a large rock on which I noticed there was a deep cross-shaped fissure. On reflection I thought of the rock, Jacob's pillow, his vision of angels on a stairway from heaven, and the words of God's promise to him that all the world would be blessed through his offspring. Jacob took the rock that he'd rested on and set it up as a pillar and called the place Bethel, or House of God, saying *Surely the Lord is in this place, and I was not aware of it . . . this is the gate to heaven.* (Gen 28:16–17).

Jesus himself fulfilled God's promise to Jacob on the cross and opened a stairway to God. He is called *the living Stone — rejected by men but chosen by God and precious to him* (1 Peter 2:4). Peter adds that believers too are living stones being built into a spiritual house. Many Scriptures picture God as the Rock in whom we can trust, and Jesus said that wise followers should build their house on the rock.

My prayer as I write is in the words of the Biblical poet: *Let the words of my mouth and the meditation of my heart be acceptable in Your sight, O Lord, my Rock and my Redeemer* (Ps 19:14).

1 2

From the Desert to Claim the Kingdom

Christ . . . lived serenely as an artist greater than all artists—
disdaining marble and clay and paint—working in living
flesh—this extraordinary artist . . . made neither statues nor
paintings nor even books—he states it loud and clear—he
made—living men, immortals.

—Vincent Van Gogh, letter to Emile Bernard, 26 June 1888

INTRODUCTION

This poetic reflection on the experience of Jesus facing temptation in the wilderness was written during the six weeks of Lent. The original purpose of Lent was identification with Christ's 40 day fast in the desert in preparation for Good Friday and Easter. I conclude each meditation with a prayer, following the pattern of the prayer the Lord taught his disciples. I enter imaginatively into the natural environment of the wilderness, while exploring the Old Testament roots of the gospel account of the temptations of Jesus. This was a time of preparation for his ministry of proclaiming the new kingdom of God in word and in deed, culminating in his death and resurrection. I end on this theme, for it is only the person of Jesus in the Gospels who can fully demonstrate life in God's kingdom and a relationship with the God of love. Recognizing and enjoying the life he gives is what *From Shore to Shore* is all about.

1. Mark 1:9–12: From the River Jordan to the Judean Desert. *Our Father.*

2. Mark 1:13: With the Wild Beasts in the Wilderness. *Your kingdom come, your will be done.*

3. Matthew 4:2–4: First Temptation: Stones into Bread. *Give us our daily bread.*

4. Matthew 4:5–7: Second Temptation: 'If you are the Son of God, throw yourself down.' *Forgive us our sins as we forgive others.*

5. Matthew 4:8–11: Third Temptation: 'All this I will give you if you bow down.' *Deliver us from evil.*

6. Matthew 4:12–16; Isaiah 9:2,7: From the Desert to Claim the Kingdom. *Yours is the kingdom, the power and the glory.*

Suggestions for reading parts when using this as a resource in public worship or group Bible study.

Reader 1: Main Narrator (Parts 1–6).

Reader 2: Old Testament quotations indicated by footnote references (Parts 1–6).

Reader 3: Words spoken by Jesus (Parts 3–6).

Reader 4: Words of Satan in the temptations (Parts 3–5).

Reader 5: Words of the mockers at the crucifixion (Part 4).

Reader 6: Prayer responses at the close of each part of the reflection (Parts 1–6).

Part 1: (Mark 1:9-12)
FROM THE RIVER JORDAN TO THE JUDEAN DESERT

Immersed in shimmering water,
the river that flows
from mountain springs
and empties
into the Sea of Death,
lowest point on earth,

you rose,
streaming with sunlight,
hearing the voice
of your heavenly Father:
This is my Son so greatly loved,
Joy of my life,

feeling the touch of the Spirit,
dove of peace alighting on you,
then like a mighty wind,
driving you out
into the wilderness,
the thirst and fasting,

leaving home comforts,
smell of fresh bread, fish cooking,
noise of hammer and hatchet,
far behind.
Alone
in the blistering heat of the sun.

No human companion
in the bleak nights.
Looking up at the vast sky,
multitude of stars—

below at your feet,
the grit and sand—

uncountable
as the children promised
to Abraham and Sarah:
She will be the mother of nations,
kings of peoples
will come from her.[9]
And here you are, one of them
in the silence
discovering more of who you are,
Promised Son,
King of Israel
and nations far beyond.

But in your isolation,
it's not an earthly crown you see
but desert thorns:
suffering humanity,
lepers, untouchables,
driven out from society—

the hungry,
the homeless,
far from family,
workbench or tools.
Then in the stillness
you listen and hear

the trickling springs of En Gedi,
whisper of wind
in the sparse, wild grass—
the voice of the Spirit

9. Gen 17:16; Gen 22:17

who has led you to this place,
words he brings to mind:

Despised and rejected,
a man of sorrows,
familiar with grief.[10]

And you know in your heart
that the path that is yours
is the path with the outcast,
for the Spirit of the Lord
is upon you
to heal the broken hearted,

set free the oppressed,
to eat with sinners
and outsiders,
welcome home the lost:
the dishonest debt collector,
exploited sex worker,
the man in chains,
the dying thief on the cross;
to embrace each one
as your brother, your sister,
release the captive
by the power of redeeming love.

Prayer:
Our Father in heaven,
Holy is your name.

May we, your sons and daughters,
honor you
by reaching out

---

10. Isa 53:3

as your Son Jesus did
to the weak, the persecuted,
the lonely,

so that in receiving from us,
they receive what you have given:
in discouragement, compassion,
in suffering, relief,
hands stretched out to welcome,
comfort in grief.

Part 2: (Mark 1:13)
WITH THE WILD BEASTS IN THE WILDERNESS

Like Adam
you dwelt with the wild beasts,
jackal, hyena, brown bear;
as you lay with a rock for your pillow
the foxes
emerged from their lair,

the vulture
that circled above you,
the viper
coiled among stones,
made nests in crevice or cavern,
you had nowhere to call your home.

Like the word you hid in your heart as a boy:
A little child shall lead,
the wolf will dwell with the lamb,
the lion on straw will feed.
They will neither harm nor destroy
for the earth will be full
of the knowledge of the Lord
as the waters cover the sea.[11]

Prayer:
Let the peace
of your kingdom come
on earth,
the justice of your will be done
in our world,
as it is in heaven

11. Isa 11:6–9; Isa 65:25

We seek your kingdom first
and desire above all else
to know you and do your will,
working for the good of humanity,
caring for the earth and all forms of life
who share this beautiful planet with us,

inspired by the hope
your word has given us,
looking to the fulfillment
of your promises:

The Lord will surely comfort Zion,
her wilderness will be made like Eden,
her wastelands like the garden of the Lord.
Joy and gladness
shall be found in her,
thanksgiving and the sound of singing.[12]

The ransomed of the Lord
will return
and sorrow and sighing
shall flee away.[13]

---

12. Isa 51:3
13. Isa 51:11

Part 3: (Matthew 4:2-4)
FIRST TEMPTATION: STONES INTO BREAD

(Setting of Temptation: desert landscape, familiar to Moses and the Israelites, and to Elijah.)

As you walked the stony desert paths,
the tracks of the ibex
and the sure-footed deer,

you retraced the footsteps of Moses—
his forty-day fast
as he waited
in the smoke of the mountain
for God's covenant to be written,

his forty-year wilderness wait
for the promised land,
with the people he led
feeding on bread
God sent from heaven;

the forty-day journey of Elijah
to a desert cave—
with only the bread
an angel once gave
sent by God to sustain him.

Feeding on the law
and the prophets' wisdom
announcing a new King coming,
in the presence of your father,
the glory of his face shining,

you saw the Word, not written on stone

but in flesh, your body given,
bread of life,
manna from heaven
sent to the world God so loved.

But in a gap in a rock
the devil was watching,
saw the stones at your feet,
the weakness of your wasting flesh,
the thinness of human bones,
the earth he wanted to destroy;

to break your spirit was his planning,
before your body was broken
to give life to the world.
He took his chance:

If you are the Son of God, he sneered,
you can turn these stones into bread.
(Just speak the word and it will appear.
Why trust in the Father and seek his will?
Achieve what is best for yourself instead).

Your voice, the voice of authority
immediately answered and said:

It is written,
Man shall not live by bread alone
but by every word that is spoken
straight from the mouth of God[14]

these words first given
to the wilderness children
with manna from heaven, their daily food,

14. Deut 8:3–4, 16–18

so the Lord would be trusted
for all that is good.

The law and the promise
you believed and upheld,
unbroken.

From the desert,
looking across the Dead Sea—
hills of Moab,
land of Jordan,
home of Ruth, your ancestor,

before she migrated
to the House of Bread,
barley fields of Bethlehem,
taking refuge under the wings
of the God of Naomi and Boaz.

What shelter,
what bread can we offer
the stranger, the multitudes
these days, in our land
and so many lands beyond?

Prayer:
Jesus, you, who knew the pain of hunger,
took the five loaves a child gave,
told disciples to feed the crowds
just as your Father had given manna
to the children of Israel,

Give us this day our daily bread
our souls and bodies need.

We receive not just a loaf,

but a harvest,
food we gather in baskets,
so much to spare, so much wasted,
food that could be gleaned.

Jesus, bread of life, broken for us,
may our lives,
your body here on earth,
be a sacramental offering
freely shared

in answer to the need and prayer
of those who hunger,
trapped in poverty,
danger, despair,

in our world
of apathy
and greed.

Part 4: (Matthew 4:5-7)
SECOND TEMPTATION: "IF YOU ARE THE SON OF GOD, THROW YOURSELF DOWN"

(Setting of Temptation: the Temple
Words quoted by Satan are from Psalm 91, a Psalm about protection in danger, associated with the Temple.)

When the sun had reached its zenith
and your throat was parched
like the dry, thirsty land,

you dwelt in the shelter of the Most High,
rested in the shadow of the Almighty,
trusted him to save you from the fowler's snare.
As he covered you with his feathers
you found refuge under his wings.[15]

All through the centuries since David
the righteous ones had sung this psalm
finding shelter in the temple
which you saw now in your mind's eye.

So Satan went with you there
to its highest point,
interrupted the words you were singing,
tried to use them to distract you from your calling:

If you are the Son of God, he said,
throw yourself down.
For it is written,

He will command his angels
concerning you,
they will lift you up in their hands
so that you will not strike your foot against a stone.

15. Ps 91:1, 3-4

Cunning darts, aimed to bring doubt:
If you are the Son of God
throw yourself down

(Why all the serving and dying?
Will God really be with you and raise you up?
Choose the fast way.
Stage the miraculous; declare your name.
Jump down.
Enjoy a spectacular moment of fame).

You focused
on the presence of your father with you
and replied,
It is written,
Do not put the Lord your God to the test,[16]

the command first given
to a wandering people
who in their thirst cried out,
Is the Lord with us
or not?[17]

The Lord on whom they could lean,
the one who led Moses to a rock
and water gushed out,
met every need,
life-giving desert stream.

You refused to test God,
doubt him in time of need,
question his love for you.

16. Deut 6:16
17. Exod 17:2–7

You believed
his faithfulness was your shield
against arrows that fly by day,
the terror of night.
You tread on the cobra.
You will trample the serpent[18]

on that dark day
when the same words will be taken,
spat like venom by soldiers to mock you
when you are dying and weak with thirst
as if God himself has forsaken you:

If you are the Son of God, come down.

And from the temple leaders
who plotted your death,
and missed the whole plot of the Kingdom:

If he is the King of Israel,
He saved others, let him save himself
and come down from the cross.

Your response
was only to your father:
Forgive them,
for they know not what they do.

And by those words
offered in that last breath
as you laid down your life for us,
we can pray:

---

18. Ps 91:4–5, 13

Prayer:
Father, forgive us,
for we have sinned against you—

Your grace and mercy
cancels debt and shame.

Father forgive us,
as we forgive others who've wronged us—
let our love in Christ be the same.

Guard our feet
from stumbling.
Lift us up
with angels' hands.[19]

19. Ps 91:11–12

Part 5: (Matthew 4:8–11)
THIRD TEMPTATION: "ALL THIS I WILL GIVE YOU IF YOU BOW DOWN"

(Setting of Temptation: a high mountain.
Jesus replies to Satan using the text of Deuteronomy, which also records the climb of Moses to the summit of Mount Nebo to view the promised land, and the last song of Moses to his people.)

You didn't allow the tantalizing words,
the destructive plot, the lies of Satan,
to stifle the song in your heart—

like the song of Moses
calling to God's servant Israel
to be faithful to the Lord,

his words glistening like dew,
raindrops on the tender herb
as the people listened:

Praise the greatness of our God!
He is the Rock, his works are perfect
and all his ways are just.
A God of truth and faithfulness.[20]

For the Lord's portion is his people,
Jacob, his inheritance.
He found him in a desert land
and in the howling wasteland
he encircled him and shielded him,
guarded him as the apple of his eye.[21]

20. Deut 32:1–4
21. Deut 32:9–10

As sand swirled around you,
you believed the words of Moses,
his last song,
relived his last mountain climb—
from the plains of Moab
to the summit of Nebo,[22]

where the Lord showed him all the lands—
from the palms of Jericho
as far as the western sea:

Waves of red-brown earth
Milk white stone
Rocks, the tint of honey
Wine-red gullies
A silver olive in a flinty crag
A hint of pastures green
Purple mist as far as eye could see
Wisp of cloud
A turquoise sky
The faint blue sea.

The land you loved too
now occupied.
Foreign troops. Extortion.
Roman forts and towers.

And the devil saw your longing
and went with you to the top of the mountain
to view the kingdoms of the world,
make a deal with you:

(Just take one step,
bow your knee to earthly power and status.

22. Deut 34:1–4

Avoid the struggle,
the sacrifice.
Submit to godless aims and values.)

All this splendor
I will give you.
If you bow down and worship me,
all will be yours.

But you would not let enticement
obstruct your clear view
of God's world:

Away from me Satan!
For it is written:
Worship the Lord your God,
and serve him only.[23]

And the devil left.

A shaft of light had flashed
into his kingdom of darkness,
shaken the stones under his feet.

He found this word God had written,
the mouth that had spoken,
unsettling,
to say the least.

A window in heaven had opened,
angels descended;
as with Jacob in the howling wilderness,
they found the Son of Man,
whom rejoicingly,
they attended.

23. Deut 6:13

Prayer:
Lead us,
let us not fall into temptation.
Deliver us from evil.

In the words of Moses in his mountain song we pray:
Like an eagle that stirs up its nest
and hovers over its young
and spreads its wings to catch them,
carry us on eagles' wings.[24]

24. Deut 32:11

Part 6: (Matt 4:12–16; Isa 9:2,7)
FROM THE DESERT TO CLAIM THE KINGDOM

Like Moses you knew God's ways,
the prophet he promised would come some day
with God's words in his mouth[25]
completing the song:

Set your heart
on the words that I give.
For by these words
you will live.[26]

Like Joshua and the people
you passed through the Jordan waters,
were tested in the desert,
but your feet did not stumble
nor your steps slip.

Ready now to step out,
life-lessons learnt,
spiritual battles won—
knowing the struggles of the poor,
the captive,

the hungry and thirsty,
the meek of the earth,
the broken hearted and weary—
to welcome them into the Kingdom
with blessing, freedom, healing, new birth.

In scorching desert sun
and in the chill of night

25. Deut 18:18
26. Deut 32:46–47

you've watched a wolf lurking,
a scorpion curled up like an egg,
a lost lamb bleating on a rocky ledge,
a lone shepherd out searching,

a man on the Jericho road
with a wounded companion,
a path, a seed, a hungry bird,
stones, scorched earth, and thorns,
scattered, shriveled seedlings,
a patch of soil—

each a Kingdom image
that you take back home
to Galilee, the way of the sea,
where you enjoy, fresh from the lake,
your first fish supper for forty days
and the delight of grapes,

to fulfill the words of the prophet:
the people living in darkness
have seen a great light;
on those living in the land of the shadow of death
a light has dawned.[27]

Ready there to call fisher-folk,
net-menders,
to follow you from the shore
and be fishers of men,
vine tenders,
shepherds laying down their lives

to feed and guard your flock
who know your voice,

27. Isa 9:2; Matt 4:16

celebrating with them
and all your people,
the yearly feast of Tabernacles,
giving thanks for fruitfulness,

olive tree and vine,
and for God's mercy
throughout their history
as tent-dwellers in the wilderness,
learning to trust in him for deliverance;
finding shelter,

God's presence in the temple,
reading from the Torah,
chanting from the Psalms
in the bright glow of the Menorah,
spring water poured on the altar—
believing what the prophets told:

The desert and the parched land will be glad,
like the crocus it will burst into bloom.
They will see
the glory of the Lord,
the splendor of our God.
Water will gush forth in the wilderness
and streams in the desert.
The burning sand will become a pool,
the thirsty ground bubbling springs.[28]

And the people at the festival dance
and sing: *Hallelu-Yah!*
Praise the Lord, all you nations,
for great is his love towards us.
Blessed is he
who comes in the name of the Lord.

28. Isa 35:1–2, 6–7

He has made his light to shine upon us.
With boughs in hand,
join in the festal procession.
Give thanks to the Lord,
for he is good;
his love endures forever.[29]

And the priest
solemnly opens and reads the scroll:
Remember your Creator
in the days of your youth.
Fear God and keep his commandments,
for this is man's all.[30]

And on the last and greatest day of the Feast
the young man filled with God's Spirit,
who suffered thirst,
overcame evil,
fulfilled the commandments,
gave his all,
opens his mouth boldly and says:

If anyone is thirsty,
let him come to me and drink.
Whoever believes in me,
as the scripture has said,
streams of living water
will flow from within him.[31]

And to the crowd listening by the lake:
I am the bread of life,
he who comes to me will never go hungry.

29. Pss 117:1–2; 118:26–27, 29
30. Eccl 12:1, 13
31. John 7:37–38

I am the living bread that came down from heaven
and gives life to the world.[32]

And to his disciples, words just before death:
If you love me keep my commands.[33]
And a new command I give you:
love one another
as I have loved you.[34]

And when he rose from the grave,
the promise unbreakable:
Go, show my Way
to the ends of the earth,
and I will be with you
day after day
right to the end of time.[35]

If you asked
would you leave
and follow another?
We would answer
like Peter,
bow and pray:

Prayer:
Lord, to whom shall we go?
You have the words of life,
real and eternal.
We believe and know
you are the Holy One of God.[36]

32. John 6:35, 51
33. John 14:15
34. John 13:34
35. Matt 28:19–20
36. John 6:67–69

Yours is the Kingdom,
the power
and the glory
forever and ever.
Hallelu-Yah.